THEOLOGY OF SOCIAL MAN

THEOLOGY OF SOCIAL MAN

by

PASCAL M. FORESI, S.T.D.
Mystici Corporis
International Institute

Translated by

JULIAN STEAD, O.S.B., S.T.L.
Portsmouth Priory
Portsmouth, R. I.

NEW CITY PRESS
148-18 85th Dr., Jamaica, New York 11435
and
2 Stamford Court, Goldhawk Road, London W. 6

First published in U.S.A. 1967
by New City Press
148-18, 85th Drive
Jamaica, N.Y. 11435

© New City Press, 1967
Library of Congress Catalog Card Number: 67-15776
Printed in Italy

FOREWORD

A lecturer in sociology, or some kindred discipline, might be embarrassed by a youth questioning his statement that man is a being who naturally lives in society. The present volume would offer some answers which are practical and alive as well as thoughtful, erudite, and penetrating.

The correlation between man and universe, individual and society, finite and infinite, accounts for certain basic tensions or " gravitations " in our nature. In these tensions lies the restlessness of man, to which this book offers solutions which are not just theoretical. The answer seems to be that man finds himself only by giving himself to others. Leaning on others makes a man less human, but union with others through giving himself completes and perfects his individuality. Society therefore should not be built upon the satisfaction of egoism so much as on the sharing of abundance.

Through work man must find his right relation to material things. He embodies his own thought in them, having first adapted it to their reality. By making him more objective, work does contribute to his perfection.

The author's manner of throwing on human life and work the light of such Christian doctrines as the fall of man, the incarnation, the role of Mary as exemplar of humanity, the future life, and — above all — the Mystical Body of Christ, cannot fail to interest reflective people who work in the fields of government, business, and labor, as well as theologians, philosophers, and sociologists. Indeed, any reader may find here stimulation to thought, life, and faith.

JULIAN STEAD, O.S.B.

CONTENTS

PREFACE

The Mystical Body of Christ is a mystery that fascinates and attracts us. It is the key to all other Christian truths, for it embraces the presence of the Trinity in Christ, the God-Man who is the Head of this Body and, in fact, of all men, for all are in some way connected with this reality.

Yet even today, this doctrine is little known. It is sad to see it rarely spoken of, and even more so to hear it described superficially, to see the part of Catholic doctrine of which the modern world stands in greatest need if it is to solve its problems, ill-treated and distorted. Other times the doctrine is presented accurately enough but coldly, lifelessly, like something memorized out of a book and having little or no connection with our day-to-day lives.

The Christian life, in reality, is not primarily an intellectual matter. To be sure, it includes dogmas and truths, and it certainly does not ask us to renounce the use of reason; but Christian revelation touches the whole of our humanity, not just the intellect. Each dogma is related to our personal lives. The mystery of the Trinity is not just a truth that can be summed up in a few formulas which, once they have been memorized, can then be left to lie idly in a corner of our minds. This mystery, the highest, most impenetrable of all, has a profoundly dynamic connection with the life of each one of us. It contains the " explanation " of our relations with our neighbor.

The same may be said about grace. The useful distinctions we learn about in books — sanctifying and actual, sufficient and efficacious grace — must not become obstacles. They point the way to a deeper comprehension of the mystery of our divine sonship, our participation in God's nature. If we live these realities, the words that express them will undergo a change: they will take on new light, become unified, and throb with a life that goes far beyond the dry and frigid definitions we once studied. Theology is life, as St. Thomas Aquinas has so wonderfully shown.

But among all the Christian truths perhaps the one that most widely and directly concerns us is that of the Mystical Body of Christ. Here is the meeting point between the human and the divine, the Trinity and creatures; men begin to live in a way that reflects the life of the Blessed Trinity. Consequently, all human realities come into contact with God. They are re-unified and led to the Father by means of Christ, His incarnate Son. The least aspect of man's life acquires new meaning, a heavenly meaning. Man's labor and his relations with others become the lobby, the anteroom, to paradise. Even our touching a thing becomes a prayer of the universe that rises to heaven.

All this, however, is so closely linked with human nature itself, as it once emerged from the hands of God, that a harmonious interlacing is formed between nature and supernature, between humanity in search of God and humanity sanctified by grace. The Church is immersed in humanity; it does not constitute an isolated class of people living on a continent of their own. Christians are the leaven of the world, and there is a profound interchange between them and non-Christians. With all other men do we share our human nature, which unites us more deeply than we think.

Every Christian is a member of humanity, of a family that he wishes to lead back to God, and to which he is socially bound, for better or for worse. Hence he suffers from the moral evil and the misery that exists in the world (and it would be so even if these were to be the afflictions only of non-believers) as from something that deeply affects him also, for it is his family, his brethren who suffer.

A Christian, therefore, cannot consider anyone on earth his enemy. He turns to every man with an open and trusting heart. To all he offers hope of redemption. However evil or violent they may be, however much they may deny God's existence, he cannot alter the doctrine in which he believes, cannot cease to love others, to try to understand them, to hope that they will once more find what they have lost.

We are all members of the same humanity, as Cicero said, and must not consider anything that is human as alien to us. But a Christian goes further: he knows that all have already been redeemed through the blood of Christ. Though they may not yet be members of His Body, they are bound to it in one way or another. After the Redemption, the bond that unites us is a much stronger and closer one than before.

Even the divisions that have plagued Christianity over the centuries, and more recently, such afflictions as secularism and communism, are sicknesses that could not have occurred before the advent of Christ. They are the maladies of Christianity. They involve our brothers who have been led astray in handling and isolating certain Christian concepts or in negating them altogether. But we must not forget that these same persons have been nourished on the milk of Christianity for generations and centuries. Whether they will it or no, in their environment they imbibe the ideas of the Christian revolution. So long as they are in good faith, they often aspire to the fulfillment of the Christian promise. That is why we Christians have a vast responsibility. If we truly believed in the Gospel, if we practiced it, many of our brothers and sisters would not now be searching outside the Church, nor reacting against it, as is often the case.

Our collective examination of conscience must be concerned with the sicknesses of mankind. The numbers of those who are not yet Christians in the world constitute an index of how much Christianity, or how much lack of it, there is in us; those who long for justice and seek it outside the Church, are the measure of how much Christian justice there is in us; those who desire a non-Christian secular world are an indication of the thirst for power that has infiltrated into our Christianity. We Christians are responsible for distorting the social countenance of Christ.

Undoubtedly each one has his personal responsibility, whether he is a believer or not. Each one could be good and has preferred not to be so. The truth is truth wherever we may find it, and error is error wherever it may be.

But how many would find God if we were better Christians?

These notes toward a theology of social man, given as weekly talks over Radio Vatican, are meant to be a modest contribution by one who believes, together with many others, that it is possible for the divine element to permeate contemporary society; that the Christianity of the Apostolic ages is by no means over; that, on the contrary, in the last centuries the Mystical Body of Christ has expanded and grown more robust. If we know how to present this reality to others through the testimony of our lives lived supernaturally, in unity of spirit, even before doing so through the apostolate of the word, today's masses will return to the Father's house. For though many are far from Him, they are always closely followed by His love.

THE AUTHOR

1 - THE TENSIONS OF MAN

To speak of man is to speak of something familiar to us all, something which comes within our immediate experience. So, too, if we ask what man is made of, anyone can supply an explanation, a definition: man is composed of soul and body. This we all repeat from childhood, from the time we learn this phrase in the first grades at school or in common speech.

It is one thing, however, to know something by heart, and another to understand it. What do soul and body mean? We are used to repeating these words, and used to thinking over their concepts so commonly, that we do not feel the need of going into them more deeply and of delving into their import. It would seem a waste of time to talk or think about them, like demonstrating that the sun really gives heat and light. Nevertheless, man — his soul, his body, and the relation between them — is one of the most unfathomable mysteries, revealing more new aspects of increasing complexity and profundity the longer we fix our attention upon it.

As we probe more deeply we face the mystery of liberty, of immortality, the mystery of man's link with God, with other men, and with nature. Man, the Fathers of the Greek Church liked to say, is a microcosm, and the whole universe is reflected and summed up in him: the spiritual universe through the soul he possesses, the material universe through his members, his flesh. Medieval philosophy, following the current of Aristotelianism, later arrived at the insight that this material part and this soul are not juxtaposed beside each other, as if constrained to live together. Although opposites, they form a harmonious whole, a new synthesis which cannot be derived from the two concepts taken separately and then added together.

Consequently, only to say that man has a soul and body is, after a fashion, to kill man; and indeed when soul and body are separated we will say that the man is dead. Man is a whole which contains both these elements, conjoined to each other intrinsically and substantially; man is the whole which is derived from the two. He is a unity, he is the " one. "

The mystery starts from here. And this is why we speak of the three *tensions* of man:

because they involve the whole man, they involve the " one. "

The first *tension* is given him by the *pondus,* the gravitation of the spiritual part of his composition. Genesis, when describing to us the formation of Adam, tells us God made him in His own image and likeness.[1] We shall never come to understand these words well enough. They mean that God constituted man outside of Himself, free to understand and to embrace the universe within man's own self, with a possibility, a power that has something infinite about it. It is a power of opening out to the attainment, though not the total comprehension, of God Himself, the Being who says of Himself: " I am the God who is." [2] He is the All, the True, the Beautiful.

Man had this spark placed in him by God, a spark that seemed to have come from the blazing fire which is God Himself. Indeed, the fact that there is spirit in us enlarges the horizon of our being, placing needs there which, it would seem, can never be satisfied. In space, it participates, in a way, in God's omnipresence, for in its mind it is able to be everywhere and

---

[1] Gen. 1, 26.
[2] Ex. 3, 14.

23

to bring everything to itself. In time, since this spark was detached from the divine fire, it too will have no end, even if it has had a beginning; it bears within itself the possibility of never dying.

Confronted by God's intelligence and God's will, as by the intelligence and will of any other being, man stands complete in himself, such that he is freely able to go or not go, do or not do, will or not will, love or not love. Indeed he is not only a piece, an individual forming part of a great universe, but he is a person, a complete " universe " in himself. This is the basis of the mysterious first *tension* of man, the first *pondus* of his nature, a *pondus* which — we underline — involves the whole being and not only his soul, even if its root is in the soul.

But man is also flesh. Here, too, we gladly return to the expression used by the Bible: " And now, from the clay of the ground, the Lord formed man, breathed into his nostrils the breath of life." [3] The material side of our composition could not have been described more plastically. The Church does not oblige us to believe that the formation of the first man

---

[3] Gen. 2, 7.

came about in the way Moses transmitted it. But, if we remove from the imagery all that may be incidental, we find underneath clearly indicated the material component of man. Man is formed of clay, of earth, and by that very fact becomes a particular thing, an individual.

Here we see the importance which the materiality of our flesh has for us: it individualizes us. One can debate St. Thomas' cosmology, bound up as it is with the Middle Ages; perhaps one can also debate certain theological conclusions of his; but he will surely remain unsurpassed in his definitive clarification of this aspect of existence which touches each one of us so closely: individualizing matter. All that we see or touch is individual. It is never a " whole. " We on this earth will never see with our carnal eyes " Man, " the plenitude of man, or the nature of man; it will always appear to us made concrete and individualized, contracted and restricted in many individuals. This is true because man is made of clay, of earth, and he carries matter in himself.

This *tension* of man toward the particular compels him to be in one place, in a determinate point of the earth in space. In time it compels him to foresee inevitably his own dissolution and death. On this account man is, of his nature, mortal. Men, by antonomasia, are defined as *mortals*.

This *pondus,* this *tension,* although rooted in matter, involves the whole compound. It involves man inasmuch as he is the " one, " since there is no other *type* man. These two mutually opposed tensions we have referred to are mysteriously linked together from the moment of our birth.

But man has yet another, a third, *tension.* He is profoundly linked to the universe in which he lives. Here, too, we find nothing more expressive than the words of Genesis: " From the clay of the ground the Lord formed man." [4] The Bible does not say that God created some clay in order to give man his materiality, but He took it from that created universe which already existed, from the cooling sphere which for millions of years had been rotating in space, perhaps after detaching itself from a star, and which man, many centuries later would call earth. He took a handful of this earth, thus constituting man not only as one of the many who were to come, but also as one of the great many things that, together with the planet on which he lived, the other stars moving in the sky and the whole universe, would give praise

---

[4] Gen. 2, 7.

to God with his own life, with his existence as a particular piece in a marvelously harmonious whole.

Man is closely linked to the material universe of which he forms a part. We are so accustomed, in thinking about men and mankind, to abstract concepts from reality, that we would almost expect that man could exist without the ground on which he walks, and even without the plants and animals on which he feeds. But in reality, since he is clay of the ground, he needs air as well as sun, soil as well as flowers, birds as well as foxes. Although he is the king of creation, he is still part of it, and profoundly bound to it. The following profound phrase of St. Thomas Aquinas, which is overlooked by so many of our books, might cause us some surprise:

> Since man is part of the corporeal universe, in the resurrection of man it is necessary that the corporeal universe should also be included; indeed, the part cannot be perfect if it remains without the whole.[5]

These three *tensions,* so opposed to one another yet synthesized in the word *man,* open up to us great horizons.

---

[5] *Compendium,* cap. 170.

2 - THE INDIVIDUAL IN SOCIETY

When talking about man, it came to us spontaneously to list the three tensions that determine him. The first, arising from his spiritual soul, drives him toward the all, the universal. The second is bound up with matter, which individualizes man and constrains him to be one among many, mortal and finite. The third tension is born of the fact that he is a part, a very tiny part, of the created universe, which, by its harmony and perfection, has sung the praise of God's glory for centuries together with the angels.

St. Augustine and his followers intuited that in these three tensions lies the profound restlessness of the human heart, which continually seeks a solution until it finally finds rest in the peace of God.

St. Thomas and the medieval scholastic realists, on the other hand, exalted and highlighted the harmonious beauty of the human creature, synthesis of the universe and symphony of opposites. The greatest contribution made by Thomism is to have clarified for us, in the footsteps of Aristotle, that soul and body do not have to be constrained to live together, as if they were both undergoing a perennial form of punishment, but are instead most profoundly united with one another. In fact, in a sense, a human being may be called " the one," just as the angels, and much more so God, may be called " one."

But how may individual men satisfy this yearning of theirs, derived from their very being, to feel themselves the all, to feel themselves " man "? Where may we find an answer to this problem, not a merely abstract and rational answer, but one that is vital and, to use a modern term, existential?

The answer that is ever more limpidly and clearly given by modern philosophy, both Christian and non-Christian, is this: a man discovers his humanity in the full sense only by giving himself to others, by living with others in society.

This makes philosophically explicit a profound truth which was already hinted at in the biblical study of Genesis. God, in fact, named the first man that He formed " Adam," that is, " man," anthropos. From him was then derived "woman," a word which translates fairly accurately the original expression in Genesis. When God formed man, he was incomplete. God then sought a complement for him, but did not find one in any animal in paradise.

Man, to be fully himself, needed to be a society, needed to be "two." This is a deep mystery that already foreshadows, though distantly, that of the Trinity itself from which it stems. Henceforth man would never be fully understood without taking into consideration this continuous tension in him toward human nature in its fullness. At the same time this human nature does not actually exist except in individuals, that is, identified in Adam, Eve, Cain, Abel, Peter and John. It is through union with individual men, therefore, that every man finds the completeness of his humanity and personality.

But it must not be thought that this need for unity with others in order to find one's self is a belittling of the individual. Here is the crux of the whole problem. Every individual is a true, responsible person in himself. The help of others, the complement of others, must be the fruit of giving, not of egoism. By leaning on others one becomes less of a man; by giving oneself to others one completes one's individuality and personality. The society that comes into being must be not so much the result of a need, as the expression of a super-abundance, a communion of goods. This is possible only because every man, while being one of many, is also, because of the spirit he possesses, complete in himself. He is a person.

Here, too, the Genesis story may serve to enlighten us. When Adam, after he had sinned, sought some justification for his act in the fact that he had been invited to rebel against God by his companion, by her who ought to have been his help, God did not accept this justification. Though Adam needed Eve in order to feel fully himself, yet he was already complete; he stood alone before God. Society is born of persons; it is not persons who are born from society.

These ideas constitute the metaphysical roots of the social nature of man. Why is society natural to man? The most recent studies of Thomism seem to supply us with the answer: it is men's actual sharing in a common nature.[1]

For this reason language and speech are special characteristics of human beings. In speech,

---

[1] Welty, *Gemeinschaft und Einzelmensch*, Salzburg, 1935.

spirit and matter combine to produce a sound that conveys a higher idea, while at the same time, speech is useless if it is not directed at another. This presupposes a plurality of persons joined together, that is, a society. Speech is the distinctive mark of man's social nature. The metaphysical foundation of this social nature resides precisely in the above-mentioned relationship between the individual and the nature of man.

But society is also natural to man for another reason, evident in the way in which God has willed that the human species should live. As soon as he is born, a child has need of someone else, a mother and a father. He needs from his very first days to find himself in a society. When he is finally grown up, having achieved a high degree of autonomy, and his powers permit him to feel self-sufficient, it would seem that he no longer needs his parents, and is at last able to detach himself in order to live a life of his own. But it is precisely then that he feels most profoundly the need to give himself to others, to form a family. And it is then that he most needs others.

Finally, when he is advanced in years and can no longer give to others, he will once again be constrained to receive, from his children and from his children's children, until kindly hands lay him with dignity into the grave, thus showing once again, in this final act, man's need to live together with other men, to commune with them, and constitute a society.

For these reasons, and because of his nature, man is under a necessity to unite with other men, to put himself in some way into them with his intellect and will. Thereby is born a moral union with them, a union that leads him to find in each person an aspect of that human nature that he needs in order to complete himself.

Already then, on the natural plane, man feels that he is one body with other men, as St. Thomas states so clearly:

> One must consider that as the different members of the body are parts of the person of the single man, so also all men are parts, or members — we might say — of human nature. For this reason Porphyry says that by sharing in the one species, many men are one. [2]

This going out to others in order to complete oneself must be verified in all men, and not only in those of one's own race and one's own time, because wherever there is a man, there will be found, as it were, a fragment of human nature. Man will find his true being by seeing himself as a small part of a particular historical moment

---

[2] *In Romanos,* cap. V, lect. III.

36

in the story of the whole human race, which, having left the hands of God as one in Adam, must also return to Him as " one."

That is why there is, intrinsic to the Christian conception of man, a philosophy, or better, a theology of history, even prior to the existence of any kind of idealistic historicism or historical materialism.

On the natural plane this unity is one of blood, as well as a moral one. No more profound bond than this is conceivable in nature.

Genesis also enlightens us regarding this need of man to find himself in humanity, to feel himself surrounded by millions of individuals and brothers. God said to Adam and Eve: " Increase and multiply, and fill the earth. " [3] Even if Adam had not brought sin into humanity, he would certainly still have established tribes and peoples. [4]

---

[3] Gen. 1, 28.
[4] " Man is by nature a social animal, therefore men even in the state of innocence would have lived socially.... This is the order which nature prescribes, because God has made man so " (*Summa Theol.* I, q. 96, a. 4).

3 - THE WORK OF MAN

Adam, and all those who followed him, had another problem to solve besides the social problem. He had to find his relationship with the universe, with things. He was, by reason of the clay out of which he had been formed, a piece of the universe, a tiny portion of it, while at the same time, he desired and aspired to be the *all,* since he was essentially *one,* as we have shown previously. He was a piece of the universe, and felt the need to relate to himself all that he saw and felt: the rivers and seas, animals and plants, precious stones and stars. From the very first moment he saw the moon, man desired to reach up to it.

God implanted this impulse in man when He joined matter and spirit together in him. For this reason the Lord turned one day to the first man and said: " Fill the earth and make it yours; take command of the fishes in the sea, and all that flies through the air, and all the living things that move on the earth. "[1] This was the external expression of all that God had already made Adam feel interiorly. He was truly the king of creation.

Man, just because he tends to be the all and to possess the all, would still have sought to transform this material universe into something similar to himself, something that bore his mark.[2]

This is why man, wherever he may be, feels the need to work upon nature and to render it his, spiritualizing it and transforming it into something that preserves the imprint of his intelligence and genius. When man sees nature in this way, in a certain sense become part of him, then he is content and satisfied, even if only for a

---

[1] Gen. 1, 28.
[2] Cf. Vatican II, *Pastoral Constitution on the Church in the Modern World,* No. 34: " Throughout the course of the centuries, men have labored to better the circumstances of their lives through a monumental amount of individual and collective effort. To believers, this point is settled: considered in itself, such human activity accords with God's will. For man, created to God's image, received a mandate to subject to himself the earth and all that it contains, and to govern the world with justice and holiness; a mandate to relate himself and the totality of things to Him who was to be acknowledged as the Lord and Creator of all. Thus, by the subjection of all things to man, the name of God would be wonderful in all the earth.

" This mandate concerns even the most ordinary everyday activities ."

moment since he will always be going out to seek new conquests.

Contact with nature itself puts man in quite a different situation from when he simply observes and contemplates it. Work certainly adds nothing essential to the nature of man. In the Middle Ages they used to say that what work adds to man is an " accident. " But what is this " accident " in reality?

When he works under the impulse of the spirit, with the guidance of his intelligence and the command of his will, man sets all of himself in motion, both soul and body. There is no intellectual work which does not entail some physical activity; and there is no manual work that does not at least imply the need for the exercise of freedom and of the intellect. Even in the most highly mechanized jobs, as in the mass production of modern factories where a worker may simply perform the act of passing an instrument or piece of machinery, repeating this act for months and years, the light of reason is always present, ever attentive and ready to intervene and correct if need be. At work under the impulse of the spirit, all our faculties are perfected and activated; they are no longer as they were before, for being has increased in them. Man in his totality feels himself more a man, simply because he is working.[3]

But this is not all. Work, every type of work, both the kind that is considered more humble by the present-day mentality and the kind that is more highly esteemed, is a participation by man in the work of creation. To be sure, this expression is not exact, since theology and philosophy use the word " creation " only with regard to Him who, from nothing, can draw the reality of being. So the word " creator " is inexactly used here; but it is used by the Fathers, the Greeks above all, to underline the grandeur of the productive activity of man.

With the agility of his hands, and the shrewdness of his calculations, man adds to being something it did not previously possess, or rather, something which previously existed only in his mind. When his work is completed, this something, now defined, perfected and realized, will exist outside of himself.

---

[3] *Ibid.* No. 35: " Just as human activity proceeds from man, so it is ordered toward man. For when a man works he not only alters things and society, he develops himself as well. He learns much, he cultivates his resources, he goes outside of himself.

" Rightly understood, this kind of growth is of greater value than any external riches which can be garnered. A man is more precious for what he is than for what he has. "

It is precisely in the course of work that man senses his greatness. We know how highly work has been exalted in different phases of the modern social revolution. At times it has even been given an absolute value, as the sole means for the elevation of man. This is the mistake of men who, seeing the product of their own hands, believe for an instant that they are wholly autonomous and powerful beings. It is an illusion destined sooner or later to collapse. But what will, perhaps, remain as a gain for the human race is the rediscovery of work as a means for perfecting man. Theologians are now undertaking a whole series of studies on this subject: theology and work, spirituality and work, asceticism and work, mysticism and work. This subject has opened a new horizon, a field that was surely not unknown before, but which now gives to work its true value as an instrument in man's development.

The reason why work actuates and elevates man is, perhaps, the fact that it constrains him to embody and to incarnate, after a fashion, that which existed in him previously only as an idea. In this act, which may seem like a descent from spirit to matter, thought must adjust itself to the reality of things. It is consequently clarified, made more distinct, illumined and verified. That which was effected by Christianity, — the union of flesh with the Word — is repeated in an analogous and remote way every time that man works and kneads matter in order to elevate it.

Yet in this act of elevation that is peculiar to work, man shows himself to be a particular piece of the universe, a part of the thing on which he works. In fact, in order to elevate it, he must lower and subject himself to it. In the course of his work he cannot prescind from the internal laws of matter; he must first discover these laws that exist outside of himself.

When the first man decided to build himself a boat in order to set out to sea, he needed to know first how logs behave in the water, and in what manner they had to be joined together so as to keep the boat afloat. In the very act by which he raises nature to himself, man must put himself at the service of inanimate nature. The medieval philosophers used to say that man, in order to reach the required end — the " finis operantis " — must subject himself, though only for an instant, to the immediate work that he does — the " finis operis. "

Work for this reason will never be for any man simply an occasion to sanctify himself, an " excuse " for drawing out of himself all his potentialities, for completing himself. Work requires an objectivity for which no act of the intelligence or the will can ever substitute since things and matter have a law of their own placed in them by God. One has to discover this law in order to abide by it. In this way, work becomes a point of encounter between humanity and things.

But once having found the right relationship with society and with things, man who is the " one " tends to return to God, gathering up in a synthesis all that he has received from His hands in order to place it humbly and lovingly at His feet. And this the very first man, Adam, could do, not only as a creature but above all as a son, since God had thus loved him from the very first instant. He had not only given him human nature, but had actually communicated to him His own divine nature, as we shall see later. Adam was truly the adopted son of God, as the Gospel of St. Luke tells us so simply: " oseph, son of Heli . . . son of Henos, son of Seth, son of Adam, who was the son of God. " [4]

And here begins the book of the genealogy of our family of workers. In Adam and Eve we were, from the very first instant, sons of God.

---

[4] Lk. 3, 23-28.

4 - MAN IN THE EARTHLY PARADISE

Many of the Fathers of the Church comment on the biblical story which relates that God breathed into man " the breath of life," [1] by telling us that in that moment God communicated to Adam not only a human soul, but also the divine nature, that which — in the terminology used many thousands of years later — is called " sanctifying grace."

Such phrases as these — " participation in the divine nature, " " elevating or sanctifying grace " — are commonplace today, although they are linked to concepts which we do not understand very often (nor do we make much of an effort to understand them).

When we use the phrase " participation in the divine nature, " we affirm the mystery of mysteries. We express the same meaning with

---

[1] Gen. 2, 7.

the term " sanctifying grace. " Subtle distinctions will never permit us to seize fully the meaning of these words.

At the moment of man's creation God deified humanity, setting before it as its end, Himself, not only as Creator, but also as Love, as Father. The divine contact with Adam's nature had an immediate effect in every dimension of his being. The breath of God penetrated his soul, reached his flesh, and thus came into contact even with the external world, with things.

Through this kiss of God within his soul, Adam at that instant contained the whole of mankind mystically within himself. One could almost say that then, though he was an individual man, he realized the dream which would henceforth remain as the constant desire of every generation: he became, in some way, " Man. " It is useless to attempt to scrutinize this affirmation too closely. We could reply to it only with another mystery, that of the Trinity. One illuminates the other while both remain, on this earth, utterly obscure to our minds. God, who is One and Threefold, one Nature in three Persons, wished to communicate something of this oneness and multiplicity to Adam. He wished him, while remaining a particular individual, to possess, in a mysterious way, the nature of all men.

Adam was thus the head of the human race, not in the sense in which the word " head " is commonly used, i. e., meaning the manager or place of management of an organism, a business or a factory; but head in the sense that he carried all mankind within himself; it was from him that all would one day receive the divine lymph. Though this relationship between Adam and humanity remains a mystery, because, as we have seen, only the mystery of the Trinity can help to throw light on it, yet it is not for that reason any less certain.

St. Paul revealed it to us in the fifth chapter of the Letter to the Romans: " One man commits a fault, and it brings condemnation upon all; one man makes amends, and it brings to all justification." [2] All of us were in Adam when he sinned. The Council of Trent affirmed that this sin is found in us not " transfused by imitation, but inherent in each one as his own. " [3]

The Lord, in giving to Adam something of Himself, obtained for him the possession of the nature of all men, this nature still remaining complete and entire in the thousands and millions of persons who would in the future be born of

---

[2] Rom. 5, 18.
[3] Denz. 790.

Adam. In this way God made it possible to resolve that natural tension in man which induces him to set up a society in order to feel himself " Man." This way of resolving and elevating that tension was something altogether superior to the needs of human nature itself. Human nature never would have dreamed of having that social tension satisfied in such a wonderful and mysterious way. Humanity thus became an image on earth of the Holy Trinity.

But the divine touch did not stop short there. Man, who is destined to die because he is made out of clay, and who is also the " one, " must be *divided* at a certain moment of his existence, for his soul is immortal, but not his body. With God's touch, Adam received the possibility of never being severed in two, of never having his flesh parted from his spirit, because a special gift of God (a gift that was bound up with his elevation to being a child of God) had changed him from mortal to immortal, even in his body. Man, therefore, who was already the " one, " would now always remain so.

But the breath of divine life that coursed through Adam also had other effects. The surrounding universe of which he was a part, acquired, through Adam, a new purpose from that very instant: to glorify God as Father. The universe acquired a supernatural end.

Nature, too, would feel this new orientation, since it now recognized in Adam its head, its chief. What riches the biblical story contains! " Take command of the fishes in the sea, and all that flies through the air, and all the living things that move on the earth. " [4] From that moment the universe of plants and animals could no longer hurt man; it could only be a help to him, a courtly ensemble for his journey to God. All the microbes that we now consider most harmful, all the animals that seem most ferocious, all the insects that we think most irritating, all of them cooperated, through a mysterious divine command, in serving man in order to serve God.

Natural human society existed in the earthly paradise, for man remained man even when raised to a supernatural level of existence. For the first family, though, civil society coincided with religious and domestic society.[5] The breath of God had not only unified the human race in Adam — while leaving individual men free —

---

[4] Gen. 1, 28.
[5] Gelasius, *De anathematis vinculo*, P.L. LIX, cols. 108-109

but it had also left the stamp of God's unity on human society, the existence of which is necessary if man is to reach God.

Humanity's contact with things through the medium of work existed even then, since the commandment to subject the earth was certainly given to man before he sinned. But work then was joyous; it was a continuation of the act of creation through the medium of the human intelligence; fatigue was unknown. Man, in continual familiarity with God, unifying all men within himself, continually rejoiced in the sweet presence of his Creator and Father, his mind illumined by God's light in order that he might live and love Him better.

Through the procreation of children, Adam would have transmitted grace, the divine nature, which was capable of unifying all things. Just as sin is proper to each of us now, according to the Church's teaching, so also would the divine nature have been transmitted to us by our parents. Wonderful consequences of the touch of God!

How many questions crowd into our mind at this point! Would men have continued forever to inhabit the earth? Would they have had the Beatific Vision? Would the Word have been made flesh just the same, in Jesus? What difference is there between our grace and Adam's, our social nature and Adam's? Would earth and sky have always remained as they are, as God created them, or would they, too, have been raised to a new sky and a new earth?

Though theology may give a partial answer to some of these problems, most of them will remain forever unanswered on this earth, for at a certain moment that wonderful paradise, that plan of infinite love which God had thought out for humanity, was rudely interrupted by an act of Adam's free will. It was only then, perhaps, that Adam realized how great he was: for he had interrupted the very plan of God. Yet God remained infinitely omniscient and immutable.

The Church does not oblige us to believe that Adam's sin consisted precisely in eating the fruit; this is something quite secondary. Putting to one side the language of Genesis — which can be either literal of figurative, though always historical — we can see that at that moment human nature in Adam, feeling itself master of all, desired to detach itself from God and put itself on a level with Him, not in order to love Him, but to put itself in opposition to Him. And then in a flash, everything vanished from his soul, from his body, and from the universe; he saw that he was only dust and clay, destined to return whence he had come.

5 – THE BREAKING OF UNITY

From the greatness to which God had raised Adam (by giving him a participation in His own nature, having made him His adopted son in a paradise of joy where he ruled as supreme being) man fell, through his sin, into a bottomless abyss of suffering. He became dust and slime again. He felt leveled down with all other creatures, infinitely distant from God, from that God with whom he had been accustomed to converse like a son.

Theology has made whole rivers of ink flow on the subject of original sin; and every heresy has sought to attack this dogma. But the words of Genesis, in their crudity, describe for us vividly the moral tragedy which man experienced at that moment: " Then the eyes of both were opened, and they realized that they were naked. "[1] They began to experience that internal

---

[1] Gen. 3, 7.

disunity from which the gifts of God had preserved them. And very soon they knew, even from God Himself, that the universe was no longer united to them as it had been formerly: work would be toil, the procreation of man would be travail, and the spirit of evil would fight continually for the downfall of the sons of men.[2]

Every aspect of man had been affected by sin. The Council of Trent says that " the whole of Adam, in soul and body, was changed to a worse state." [3] This means the whole of man, with all his tensions: those which lead him to the infinite, the all, to God; and those which lead him to unite himself with men and with creation. The universe which had been unified, became dislocated onto different planes, still linked to one another but each henceforward instinctively tending to its own particular good; concupiscence in man means exactly that. Man will be obliged to live in a world in which he had once been *all* and *one*; but now he is divided and partial. The consequences of sin on the social plane were terrible. Brothers will henceforth seek each other out not to give themselves to one another, but to kill each other. This is the story of Cain which is found in the history of the first family.

---

[2] Gen. 3, 14-19.
[3] Denz. 788.

When the family grew into a people, mutual incomprehension inevitably spread. Speech had been for Adam a special gift of God, the medium for union among the first men, helping them even after their sin, making them feel that they were somehow still united. Speech suddenly became the symbol and sign of division among men. Work, which had previously been a means of raising things to oneself in order to lead them to God, and a means of getting others to cooperate in building the new society, became the beginning of division among men and made it possible for man to use nature in order to go against God. But, for this attempt man will be condemned by God. Let us recall the biblical story which tells us of the dispersal of the peoples:

Hitherto, the world had only one way of speech, only one language. And now, as men traveled westwards, they found a plain in the land of Sennaar, and made themselves a home there; Here we can make bricks, they said to one another, baked with fire; and they built, not in stone, but in brick, with pitch for their mortar. It would be well, they said, to build ourselves a city, and a tower in it with a top that reaches to heaven; we will make ourselves a great people, instead of scattering over the wide face of earth. But now, God came down to look at the city, with its tower, which Adam's children were building; and He said, Here is a people all one, with a tongue common to all; this is but the beginning of their undertakings, and what is to prevent them carrying out all they design? It would be well to go down and throw confusion into the speech they use there, so that they will not be able to understand each other. Thus God broke up their common home, and scattered them over the earth, and the building of the city came to an end. [4]

The very first work which man accomplished on earth became the symbol of God's malediction. This is a scene which ought to be meditated upon profoundly, inasmuch as we will later meet once again the image of the peoples and languages. The day of Pentecost will remind us of the day of Babel, just as the united canticle of the peoples before the throne of God, in the Apocalypse, will remind us of the story of man, of the dispersal of those who erected a tower with their hands that would enable them to reach up to heaven.

God's malediction because of men's sin fell on all created things. In the Bible other creatures are much more closely bound up with men than we are nowadays accustomed to think. Scripture says:

And now God found that earth was full of men's iniquities, and that the whole frame of their thought was set continually on evil; and he repented of having made men on the earth at all. So, smitten with indig-

---

[4] Gen. 11, 1-9.

nation to the depths of his heart, he said, I will blot out mankind, my creature, from the face of the earth, and with mankind all the beasts and the creeping things and all that flies through the air; I repent of having made them. [5]

God sees the whole universe bound up with man, sharing in his ruin or in his glory. This connection with nature might be attributed by some to the antique use of rather anthropomorphic language, due to the roughness of the hearts of those to whom Moses' message was directed. But is it not rather we, perhaps, who fail to understand certain things, because our hearts have lost the simplicity needed to intuit the exact value of the gifts of God?

If after the first sin, man — using only his own powers — had allowed every aspect of his nature to develop, the world and the universe would have increasingly presented a picture of anguish and desperation. With the evolution of mankind and of nature, disunity and conflict would have continued to multiply, introducing incurable inner disharmony within individual men precisely because man is, in a sense, a part of all: a part of the spiritual world, of humanity, and of things.

This is the same anguish that is experienced even now by those who are without God. But

---

[5] Gen. 6, 5-7.

at the very instant when the sentence was pronounced on Adam and Eve in the terrestrial paradise, the Lord Himself presented mankind with the hope of a solution, the hope of the restoration of unity. Certainly when Adam and Eve learned from God Himself of the offspring to come that would crush the serpent's head (the spirit of evil), they did not fully comprehend the infinite love contained in the words of the Most High.

In the course of the ages the image of the Liberator, the Reconstructor of lost unity, was gradually sketched, as with the touches of a brush on a painting. But however confusedly or obscurely God's promise was transmitted to posterity, new revelations preserved, expanded, and purified it not as a reality but as a hope of the One who would one day come to " recompose " the universe. God again gave men the grace to return to Him, to prepare a place worthy of receiving Him on this earth.

Thus we have a whole series of pictures and real facts, of revelations and prophets, which were preparing humanity and reconstructing the peace within a chosen people, a people which would be the symbol and figure of a reality to come. The priesthood, the king, the sacrifice, the temple, the enemy — named

Babylon — the sacraments, the rites, the first fruits of nature: all these things were realities vital for the men of that age, while at the same time they were signs of much greater things to be realized in the last days. These signs at times signify the final restoration at the end of the world, and at times they point to mankind's period of trial after the coming of the Messiah.

The images are superimposed on each other and interlaced to such a degree that, even now, we ourselves are not always able to understand and distinguish them.

In this time of longing, which is both a symbol and a reality, humanity continually struggles against the forces of dispersal let loose in the world by original sin, and constantly builds what will later be once again destroyed by the wicked. Meanwhile the day approaches when it will be made worthy to receive through one of its own, an entirely pure and beautiful creature, the Liberator and definitive Re-unifier: Jesus, the One, in the highest sense of the word.

6 - THE REUNIFICATION OF THE COSMOS IN CHRIST

Theologians have asked themselves in how many ways God could have healed the sin of Adam, and they have almost unanimously agreed that this could have been effected in many ways:[1] for example, by showing mercy — which simply forgets all and restores man to the state of innocence, or by means of some chosen prophet, who might, perhaps, have been preserved from sin.

These different solutions would clearly have had different effects on mankind. God was free, entirely so. But in His infinite love for men, by a mysterious decree of the Blessed Trinity, it was decided that man would be redeemed in a way absolutely unthinkable to us: God Himself would assume the task of paying the debt of sin, but not with an act made outside of the

---

[1] St. Thomas, *Summa Theol.* III, q. 46, a. 2, ad 3.

human race. He would actually become a creature.

The Trinity's decree of the Incarnation is a mystery that can never be completely plumbed. We would like to suggest, however, a few thoughts for meditation.

We are often led, by the language we use, to form an inexact idea of what happened at Nazareth at the moment when the angel announced to the Blessed Virgin that the Word was to become flesh. We are led by an anthropomorphic mentality to think of God far off, high up in the skies, sending His Son to be made man in a distant, wild place. Not so; God is everywhere, in heaven, on earth, in every locality. So God was in the Virgin's little room at Nazareth when the angel appeared to her. He was at the same time, however, infinitely distant from His creatures by reason of the abyss of sin, and also because of their natural smallness.

The instant that the Virgin pronounced her *fiat,* God espoused human nature to Himself in her pure womb; He espoused the creature, causing the deity and the universe to approach one another in a manner beyond our imagination. Ever since then, He has been in our midst. The infinite distance that our imagination conjured up, putting God far off above the skies, has been canceled out: He is on earth, as our fellow citizen.

The center of the universe is the Trinity: from then on the Trinity is present in a man. The Incarnation, seen through the eyes of God, is actually the work of the whole Trinity, even if only the second divine Person, the Word, is the terminus of the assumption of human nature. It is the Trinity itself that dwells in Christ, because of the inseparable unity of the divine nature.

At that moment, in Christ, God brought about a new centralization and orientation. If the stars, billions of light-years away, had had eyes, they would have fixed them upon Mary, who bore the Creator in her womb.

It has been observed by the Fathers of the Church that the most complete synthesis imaginable came about at that moment. They say in their writings that the divine Person of the Word, who assumed human nature, is in some way a synthesis of the Trinity, both because He is begotten of the Father, and because the Holy Spirit is breathed from Him in union with the Father. Christ, moreover, in taking a human nature, assumes nature itself, a synthesis of all creation. Man in fact, though inferior to the angels through having a body, is a unity possessing something of every order of things: there are minerals, like iron and calcium, in him; the vital processes of plants are present in him; he also has the typical sensations of the animals and a spiritual nature in common with angels. Man is a microcosm, the Church Fathers repeatedly say, a summary of all things. Henceforward Christ constitutes a new unity, summing up in Himself the fullness of divinity and humanity — not, mind you, as two juxtaposed realities only morally connected with each other, but most profoundly united, substantially and hypostatically. There is only one Person in the two natures.

This contact with mankind and with created things in the Person of Jesus was reflected directly on all mankind and the whole universe from the first moment of the Incarnation.[2] At that

---

[2] " On that account, echoing in spiritual harmony all the ages of the Christian era, we venerate the Redeemer of the human race, not as ' *Elias . . . or one of the prophets* ', in whom the divinity dwells through grace, but joining our voice to that of the prince of the Apostles, who knew this mystery by divine revelation, we confess: ' *You are the Messiah, the Son of the Living God* ' (Matt. 16, 16).

" Having ensured this dogmatic truth, we can easily deduce from it that *the universal family of men and of created things has been raised by the mystery of the incarnation to such dignity that certainly none greater could be imagined, a dignity definitely more sublime than that to which it was raised by the work of creation.* For this way there is one among the descendents of Adam, namely Christ, who reaches even as high as the celestial and infinite divinity, and is united with it in a mysterious and

moment Jesus' soul, being united to the divinity, received a grace so great that it was itself the source of every other grace: at that instant Jesus became the Head of the human race.

In theology this grace is called the "gratia capitis." Through this grace all of us, though still needing to be redeemed, became spiritually united in Jesus. Our social nature was going back once more from the natural social nature to that which is supernatural, and was even entering into the very sphere of the Trinity. We became members of the Body of the Son.

These are the words of Pope Saint Pius X, concerning our mysterious presence in Jesus:

> In the very womb, therefore, of His most pure Mother, Christ took flesh and, at the same time, united a spiritual body to Himself, formed of those " who would find faith in Him." In this sense one could say that Mary, when she bore the Savior in her womb, bore too all those whose life was contained in that of the Savior. All of us, therefore, who are united with Christ, and — in the words of the Apostle — are "members of His body, of His flesh and of His bones " (Ephesians 5, 30), came forth from the womb of Mary, by analogy, with a body united to its Head. [3]

---

exceedingly close manner; Christ we say, Who is truly our brother, endowed with human nature, but is also God with us " (Pius XI, *Lux veritatis, A.A.S.* 1931).

[3] Pius X, *Ad diem illum laetissimum,* A.A.S., 36, pp. 452-453. So Pope Paul VI has pronounced Mary " Mother of the Church."

Theologians ask themselves how we could have been present in Jesus even before the Redemption. It must be recognized that this presence was not complete until the passion and death of Jesus: only then did He become our Head effectively.[4] But the ontological foundation was there from the moment that Mary gave her assent.

The social nature of man which had been raised up in Adam by grace, received a new and higher elevation in Christ: the human nature of each of us was present in Him even before we were born, when we still needed, by faith and baptism, to accept our insertion into the Body of Christ.

Of this there can be no exhaustive, rational explanation. It is the mystery of the Trinity which begins to pour its rays and its dark luminosity on the creature in direct contact with the Word, in other words, upon the human nature of Jesus. Though a man, He re-assumes all of us, and He re-assumes us even before we have been redeemed.

In connection with the quotation from Pope Saint Pius X, the reader is urged to read Nos. 55, 56, and 60-62 of Vatican II's *Dogmatic Constitution on the Church*.

[4] Cf. Dictionnaire de Théologie Catholique, vol. XIII, col. 1983.

Already at that moment Jesus recapitulated all things. As Cajetan says, " The Incarnation is a raising of the whole universe up to the divine Person. " [5]

St. John Damascene, whom we quote here as a sample of the whole Greek tradition which has produced many marvelous pages on this mystery, says:

> The benign will of the Father worked the salvation of the entire world in His only-begotten Son, and established a unification of all things. In fact, as man bears in himself the weft and the bond of every nature, visible and invisible, the Lord, Creator and Ruler of all things, willed that the union of the divinity with humanity be established in His only-begotten and consubstantial Son, and thereby the union of all things, so that God might be all in all. [6]

And, again, the same Father affirms, " What has not been assumed has not been saved. " [7]

Even material things were present, recapitulated, in Jesus at the Incarnation; in Him at Bethlehem they recovered a supernatural meaning and purpose.

This recapitulation of all things in Christ — first and in a special way, of humanity, but

---

[5] *In IIIm,* q. 1, a. 1, n. 7.
[6] *Orat. de Transfig. Dom.,* n. 18.
[7] *De Fid. orth.* Bk. III, chap. VI.

also of material things — is not due to God's arbitrary decree. It was the logical consequence of the natural bond between men: if one member of humanity came into this kind of contact with God, it was impossible for him not to become Head of the human race. Consequently, when man was created with a social nature, in the mind of God this social nature would have already appeared as raised up by Christ. The same would have been true of material things: man is not just a separate human creature, but is a part of the universe which has entered into contact of a profound kind with God Himself, in the unity of one Person.

The entire universe, as a result of this, feels in Jesus the effect of the immense honor that has been bestowed upon it.

7-THE MYSTERY OF THE AGES

Why did Jesus want to suffer and die for us? Theology teaches that the slightest suffering on His part would have been sufficient to redeem the human race from all its sins.[1] The liturgy repeats the same theme when it sings: " Jesus, Lord, loving pelican, cleanse me, the unclean, with Thy blood, only one drop of which can save the whole world from all crime." Pope Clement VI confirms the same, *ex cathedra,* when he declares: " Immolated innocently on the altar of the cross, Christ did not shed just one drop of blood, which, by its union with the Word, would have been enough for the redemption of the whole human race, but poured it out copiously as if it were a river of blood." [2] But why, then,

---

[1] Cf. St. Thomas, *Summa Theol.* III, q. 46, a. 5 ad 3.

[2] Denz. 550 — Bull *De satisfactione Christi et thesauro Ecclesiae.*

did He take death upon Himself to expiate our guilt?

We have already seen that Jesus, through the *gratia capitis,* is Head of humanity and of all things from the moment of the Incarnation. But of what sort of humanity is He the Head? Having chosen to assume the flesh of Adam, in the Incarnation He became Head of a humanity whose members are " criminals, " as Louis Chardon, theologian and mystic of the 17th century, assert in the book *La croix de Jésus.* [3]

---

[3] " But since, moreover, this grace was given Him for the very reason for which He descended to the world, and because the function He must perform in the world concerns the reparation He must make as Head for His criminal members, one must conclude that this abundance of grace gave His soul a disposition and inclination to obey the decree made in the counsels of the most glorious Trinity, including the cross, with all the other terrifying circumstances proper to the performance of strict reparation.

" Those who are wise teach that grace disposes one for the ministry to which one is called; reason indicates this, and the Scriptures inspired by the Holy Spirit also teach it. But that Jesus, as Head of His Mystical Body, has an obligation to make satisfaction for His members, and to save His mystical person in His mystical members, in order to fulfill David's prophecy: 'You have ransomed from Egypt the people and its God' (2 Kings 7, 23)... of this we say that the Son of God, speaking absolutely and considering Him in His own person, could not, before or after the Incarnation, have had any obligation to make reparation for us; only His charity and His pure mercy were the cause of His becoming man, and He became the Redeemer of the world only for these reasons.

" He offered Himself, says the Prophet (Is. 53, 7) ' because it was his own will.' Nevertheless, since He constituted and

He did not have original sin because He preserved the blessed Virgin Mary and Himself from that stain. But as St. Thomas says, He willed to take upon Himself something of the state of degeneration into which we men had fallen. " He assumed, of the sinful state, the necessity of undergoing the penalties of this life," says the *Summa Theologica*.[4] Jesus freely assumed a nature of this kind, whereas He could have had one which was perfect. Once it was assumed, He subjected Himself to the necessary consequences of His choice.

Again St. Thomas, commenting on a phrase of St. Paul to the Romans, tells us: " He did not actually have the flesh of sin, i.e., conceived with sin, because His flesh was conceived by means of the Holy Spirit who takes away sin; but it had the likeness of the flesh of sin, i. e., of sinful flesh, insofar as it was possible." [5] The Angelic Doctor says, " Christ assumed human

---

established Himself as head of the faithful souls belonging to His grace, and since He has made them one same Person with Himself in His Mystical Body, He contracts the duty to make reparation for the members who have offended; just as the head, although it is healthy and free from sickness, is concerned with the cure of the other members of its body, and just as the face of someone of good family is covered with shame and suffers confusion when another member commits some disorder against the honor to which he lays claim " (Louis Chardon O. P. *La croix de Jésus,* Paris, 1937, pp. 46-47).

[4] *Summa Theol.* III, q. 13, a. 3 ad 2.
[5] *In Romanos,* cap. VIII, lect. 1.

defects in order to make reparation for the sin of human nature . . . . Christ, then, had to assume those defects which are a consequence of the common sin of the whole of nature, but which nevertheless are not incompatible with the perfection of His knowledge and His grace." [6]

There is one moment in the passion in which all the profound meaning of the suffering of Jesus becomes apparent. It is precisely when He cries: " My God, my God, why hast thou forsaken me? " [7] This is the sorrow which gives a particular bitterness to all the sufferings of Jesus on the cross.

St. Augustine comments: ". . . Christ speaks thus, because Christ is in the members of Christ." [8] The holy Doctor asks himself: " Why did Christ say, ' My God, my God, why hast thou forsaken me? ' if not because we were there, and because the Church is the Body of Christ? " [9] On the cross Jesus " was our voice, because together with Him our old man was crucified."[10] " Christ says these things in the person of His body, which is the Church . . . . Therefore, why

---

[6] *Summa Theol.* III, q. 14, a. 4 in c.
[7] Mk. 15, 34.
[8] *Enarrat. in Psalm.* 31, P. L. 36, 231.
[9] *Enarrat. in Psalm.* 21, P. L. 34, 172.
[10] *Enarrat. in Psalm.* 70, P. L. 36, 882.

should we disdain to hear the voice of the Body from the mouth of the Head? In Him the Church was suffering when He suffered for the Church; as He, too, was suffering in the Church whenever the Church has suffered for Him. In fact, as we heard the voice of the Church suffering in Christ say, ' My God, my God, why hast thou forsaken me? ' so too, we heard the voice of Christ suffering in the Church exclaiming, ' Saul, Saul, why persecutest thou me? ' " [11]

Augustine's interpretation is taken up by Thomas Aquinas. The great bishop of Hippo had remarked that the sins are ours, the passion is Christ's; St. Thomas remarks that Jesus in that cry spoke " in the person of sinners who sometimes are forsaken because of their sins "; and again: " . . . things which refer to the members Christ says of Himself, inasmuch as Christ and the Church are as only one mystical Body, and hence they speak as only one person, and Christ transforms Himself into the Church and the Church into Christ." [12]

To sum up, this cry can only be explained by keeping in mind the mystery of the Mystical Body, understanding that the suffering of Jesus was the penalty for humanity's sin.

---

[11] *CSEL,* VI, 18, 168-169.
[12] *In Psalmos David expositio,* 21, Romae MDLXX.

For St. John of the Cross this cry of abandonment is the supreme moment of the passion, the revelation of the meeting between humanity, united to Jesus, and God. The great mystic explains:

> As for His spirit, it is certain that in His last moments (Jesus) suffered also an annihilation of the soul, the Father leaving Him without any consolation or comfort, in the deepest aridity of the soul's interior region; so much so that on the cross He burst into that grief-stricken cry: My God, my God, why hast thou forsaken me? This was the greatest pain He sensibly experienced in His mortal life. So it was that at that very moment He completed the greatest of all the works He ever did in His life, greater than all the miracles and sensational prodigies He performed on earth or in heaven: the work through which He reconciled and united man to God by means of grace. [13]

The theologian Pietro Parente sums up the traditional teaching in his statement that Christ's suffering culminates on the cross when He makes use of that verse of the twenty-first psalm, " My God, my God, why hast thou forsaken me? " to reveal its convulsive climax. [14]

By His passion and death, suffering the effects of the curse within Himself, [15] Jesus

---

[13] *Ascent of Mount Carmel,* Bk. II, chap. 6.
[14] *Teologia viva,* vol. I: *Il mistero di Cristo,* Roma, 1954, p. 157.
[15] *Gal.* 3, 13.

opened the gates of paradise to mankind and the universe. Hence it was only with His death on the cross that He became Head of the Church in the full sense of the word. [16]

At this point, imagination could lead us to think that heaven was far from Christ when He was redeeming us on the cross; and yet we know that the Trinity and our Lord were inseparably " one " for all eternity.

When he opened divine life to humanity, He manifested Himself. He is heaven for us. Henceforward it is up to us as individuals to find our place in the Body of Christ, accepting our incorporation in order to enter into and enjoy the face-to-face vision of the Trinity, as " sons in Him, the Son. "

This hidden mystery of the Passion is revealed by St. Paul in his letter to the Colossians (a small community in a town of Asia Minor which owes its fame to the Apostle). He revealed to these simple people that all things were recapitulated in Christ at His passion:

> He is the head whose body is the Church, It begins with Him, since His was the first birth out of death; thus in every way the primacy was to become His. It was God's good pleasure to let all completeness dwell in Him, and through Him to win back all

---

[16] Cf. S. Tromp S. J., *Corpus Christi quod est Ecclesia*, Roma, 1946, p. 77.

things, whether on earth or in heaven, into union with Himself, making peace with them through His blood, shed on the cross.[17]

As every order of things in the universe was mystically included in Christ at the Incarnation, so they all recovered unity with God on the cross. St. Jerome in his commentary on St. Paul's Epistle to the Ephesians says:

All the economy which preceded the universe and which later was established in the world, for creatures invisible and visible, foretold the coming of the Son of God . . . . Therefore it was on the Lord's cross and in His passion that all things were recapitulated, everything being reassumed in this recapitulation . . . . All mysteries and all the old economy of earth and of heaven were fulfilled in the passion of Christ. Since Christ has suffered for me, was buried, has risen and ascended victoriously to heaven, I have no more need of the ancient things: in one alone I possess all. And mark well, not only the earthly happenings reported to us in the Sacred Scriptures by the Holy Spirit, but also the heavenly events which are still hidden from us, were recapitulated in the passion of Christ.[18]

The social nature of man could not have performed a greater role in the drama of the universe. It is the key which lets in a ray of light upon the mystery of Calvary.

---

[17] Col. 1, 18-20.
[18] *Commentarium in epistulam ad Ephesios I*, P.L. 26, 454.

8 - THE CHURCH: CHRIST'S BODY

In the course of tracing briefly the history of the social nature of man, we have seen that the noblest chapter in the story, the most sublime encounter, is the meeting with Christ: when God Himself made use of the social tension inherent in man to raise the family of mankind to new heights. In Christ, in fact, man shares in the Trinitarian life itself, which is the social life of God.

This supernatural communion, however, which the life of grace has brought to men, does not destroy natural life. On the contrary, the two are marvelously interwoven. The life of supernatural communion, the life of grace, brings about and makes possible a social life that is complete even on the natural plane, since it was a visible Church that Christ founded. While, at the same time, it is the visible Church which, through human relations and tangible symbols

— the sacraments — allows every Christian to share in the mysterious, invisible communion which is the supernatural life.

But what is the point of transition from Christ to the Church? How does one pass from the spiritual presence of humanity in Christ to the presence of Christ in humanity? To comprehend this we must contemplate the human nature of Jesus, both before His death and after His resurrection. We must meditate on His individual physical being which, after its exaltation, became life-giving. Then we shall see how, at the moment when Jesus rose from the dead, the community of His disciples received the Holy Spirit and thus became the Church where Christ is present. The members of the Church became, mystically, members of His Body.

Jesus gave us a glimpse of this truth when He spoke of the Eucharist in the discourse recorded by St. John in the sixth chapter of his Gospel. The Jews were scandalized because Jesus had asserted that eternal life could be obtained by eating His flesh and drinking His blood. He went on to say: " Does this try your faith? Only the spirit gives life; the flesh is of no avail." [1] Jesus is here referring to His future

---

[1] Jn. 6, 61-63.

spiritualization, when His body will still be a true body, but will acquire the sanctifying powers of the spirit.

Before His crucifixion, the radius of activity of Christ's humanity was limited by His sensible mortal flesh; with His death and resurrection it becomes life-giving spirit. St. Hilary said: "Christ is the Church through the mystery of His body which contains the whole Church in itself." [2] And St. Cyril of Alexandria asserted: " We are a body because He has incorporated us into a Body, i. e., His own, as concorporeal with Him." [3]

For this reason, on the glorious day of Easter Sunday, when the Spirit penetrated and illumined every part of the body of Jesus, the Church, too, received the Holy Spirit; it became the Body of Christ. We can say that Christ sowed a particular body and then rose as the Mystical Body, as the Church. [4]

The mystery of man's social nature, therefore, is much in evidence in these marvelous events. Since Christ wished to be a member of the human community, He became its Head. So, when He suffered on the cross, He redeemed the human race since it is spiritually included in Him. Even His individual flesh — by the

---

[2] *Enarrat. in Psalm.* 125, 6.
[3] *In Joh.* 11, 11 P. G. 74, 560.
[4] Durwell, *La résurrection de Jesus,* Lyon, 1961, p. 220.

assumption of which He chose to effect the work of the Redemption — acquires certain dimensions of infinity. It is spiritualized and becomes the very image of a new humanity. For Jesus after the Resurrection, the flesh, which is a principle of limitation in man, becomes a means for the universalizing of life.

But let us continue with our inquiry. What exactly does " Mystical Body of Christ " mean? In a broad sense, on the cross the whole human race became the Mystical Body of Christ " inasmuch as all men belong to Christ as a reality to be saved by the Redeemer." [5]

This expression, interpreted broadly, already points to a profound reality. It is enough to remember that the Resurrection of Christ is the efficient cause of the resurrection of the body of every man: of those who will one day belong to the Church, as well as of those who will never know of it; of the good and of the bad. [6]

---

[5] Pietro Parente, *De Verbo Incarnato,* Roma 1956, p. 347, footnote.

[6] " As the other things Christ did or suffered in His humanity are salutary for us by virtue of His humanity... so also Christ's resurrection is the efficient cause of our resurrection through His divine power, a characteristic of which is the capacity to raise the dead to life. The latter power reaches into all places and all time with its presence, and extends not only to good men but also to the bad ... " (St. Thomas, *Summa Theol.* IIIa. q. 56, art. 1 ad 3).

The expression "Mystical Body of Christ," however, in its more precise and definite sense, signifies the Church, which is an extension here on earth of the work of Christ Himself.

At this point, further doubts may arise concerning the full meaning of the phrase "Mystical Body." Is it such an abstract and utterly mysterious thing that no one knows for sure who it is that belongs to it, or does it stand for something clearly identifiable?

Bringing the exposition of all our preceding chapters to a logical conclusion, we here draw a clear inference: if the Mystical Body is made up of men, then it is a human society. It is a reality that flows from the need God placed in man at the very moment of his creation. It must consequently possess all the marks of true society, for otherwise, this Christian reality would not include man as he is, with all the tension in which he finds his fulfillment. The life of grace is grafted onto human nature, and when this life constrains men to join together, as in the case of the Church — the Mystical Body — the resultant society will also need to be humanly perfect.

So we find that, in the slow deepening of our comprehension of revelation, the expression "Mystical Body of Christ" has now got to be attributed exclusively to that complete human and divine society which is the Catholic,

Apostolic, Roman Church. In the encyclical *Humani Generis,* Pope Pius XII says that we must firmly maintain the Catholic Church to be a reality identical here on earth with the Mystical Body of Christ. He, in fact, reproves those who " do not consider themselves bound by the doctrine which we expounded in one of our encyclicals (*Mystici Corporis*) and which is founded on the sources of revelation, according to which the Mystical Body of Christ and the Roman Catholic Church are one and the same thing. " [7]

---

[7] Pius XII, *Humani Generis,* 1950. This paragraph must be read in the light of the following quotation from Vatican II, *Decree on Ecumenism* No. 3: " From her very beginnings there arose in this one and only Church of God certain rifts (cf. 1 Cor. 11:18-19, Gal. 1:6-9; 1 Jn. 2:18-19), which the apostle strongly censures as damnable (cf. 1 Cor 1:11 ff.; 11:22). But in subsequent centuries more widespread disagreements appeared and quite large Communities became separated from full communion with the Catholic Church — developments for which, at times, men of both sides were to blame. However, one cannot impute the sin of separation to those who at present are born into these Communities and are instilled therein with Christ's faith. The Catholic Church accepts them with respect and affection as brothers. For men who believe in Christ and have been properly baptized are brought into a certain, though imperfect, communion with the Catholic Church. Undoubtedly, the differences that exist in varying degrees between them and the Catholic Church — whether in doctrine and sometimes in discipline, or concerning the structure of the Church — do indeed create many and sometimes serious obstacles to full ecclesiastical communion. These the ecumenical movement is striving to overcome. Nevertheless, all those justified by faith through baptism are incorporated into Christ. They

Already in 1595, Clement VIII taught the same thing clearly in a bull in which he sanctioned the reunion of the Ruthenian Church with Rome. The Pope praised the fact that the Archbishop of Kiev, " and the majority of the bishops of his province, their hearts illumined by the Holy Spirit, began to think among themselves, having consulted each other over a long period of time prudently and seriously, that they and the flocks which they fed were not members of the Body of Christ which is the Church, because they were not united with the visible head of the same Church, the Roman Pontiff . . . ." [8] And St. Augustine, as early as the 4th century, stated: " Only the Catholic Church is the Mystical Body of Christ. " [9]

---

therefore have a right to be honored by the title of Christian, and are properly regarded as brothers in the Lord by the sons of the Catholic Church. "

[8] Clement VIII, *Magnus Dominus,* X, December 23, 1595.

[9] *Ep.* 185, 50 P. L. 33, 815. Cf. also Vatican II, *Decree on Eastern Catholic Churches,* No. 3: " Such individual Churches, whether of the East or of the West, although they differ somewhat among themselves in what are called rites (that is, in liturgy, ecclesiastical discipline, and spiritual heritage) are, nevertheless, equally entrusted to the pastoral guidance of the Roman Pontiff, the divinely appointed successor of St. Peter in supreme governance over the universal Church. They are consequently of equal dignity, so that none of them is superior to the others by reason of rite. They enjoy the same rights and are under the same obligations, even with respect to preaching the gospel to the whole world (cf. Mk. 16:15) under the guidance of the Roman Pontiff. "

These papal affirmations certainly are not intended to mean that outside of the Catholic ecclesial society there cannot be a real, even if incomplete, grafting into Christ and His Church. Much light has been shed in this regard by the documents of the Second Vatican Council which, although confirming the traditional doctrine that " Mystical Body = Catholic Church," have, on the other hand, presented a broader and more complete vision of both these terms.[10]

Having followed, step by step, the inherent logic of the Incarnation in which God willed to make a marvelous union of the divine and the human, Catholic teaching is clear and convincing on this point: just as Christ, the Son of God, was true and perfect man, so the Mystical Body is

---

[10] " This is the unique Church of Christ which in the Creed we avow as one, holy, catholic, and apostolic. After His Resurrection our Savior handed her over to Peter to be shepherded (Jn. 21:17), commissioning him and the other apostles to propagate and govern her (cf. Mt. 28, 18 ff.). Her He erected for all ages as ' the pillar and mainstay of the truth ' (1 Tim. 3:15). This Church, constituted and organized in the world as a society, subsists in the Catholic Church, which is governed by the successor of Peter and by the bishops in union with that successor, although many elements of santification and of truth can be found outside of her visible structure. These elements, however, as gifts properly belonging to the Church of Christ, possess an inner dynamism toward Catholic unity " (Vatican II, *Dogmatic Constitution on the Church*, No. 8).

fully and perfectly human as well as divine. The Incarnation continues to produce its effects daily until the end of the ages, through the visible Church.

9 - THE MARKS
OF THE CHURCH

In the last chapter we saw briefly how the Church, the Mystical Body was born from the cross itself (from Jesus' rib, say the Fathers). Christ dies on the cross and then rises in His own body and, spiritually, in those that had followed Him, those who had formed with Him the first community of disciples. No longer are they a sparse group dispersed by terror, but a recollected assembly at prayer; they are now the Mystical Body of Christ. The events of Pentecost will later bring the crowning reward of the presence of the Holy Spirit; but these souls are already " with one mind giving themselves up to prayer, together with Mary the mother of Jesus. " [1]

This little group, which is already the Mystical Body of Christ in the full sense, expands little by little as the days go by. Its membership

---

[1] Acts 1, 14.

grows from hundreds to thousands, first in Jerusalem, then in Samaria, Antioch, Cyprus, Iconium, Rome, and all over the world.

They are men just like the rest, but as a common characteristic they have something divine which marks them out from the world; as Jesus said, they are " in the world but not of the world." [2] They are like others in that they share the sufferings, the liability to sin, and the mortality of the descendants of Adam; but they are not of the world, because something lives in them which transcends them: the mystical presence of Jesus. Together with Him they form one mystical Person. Each is an individual and is free, but is, just the same, penetrated by this mysterious presence.

Considering this reality from the social point of view, we see that although these individuals together form a multitude, yet they are united among themselves in such a way that the society they form is not even remotely comparable to any earthly society. In addition, this group of people has qualities, characteristics, derived precisely from the fact that there is Someone present in their midst.

These characteristics are also evident externally; Jesus is present in real, concrete people,

---

[2] Jn. 17, 11-14.

and He therefore produces effects in them that are humanly verifiable and sociologically determinable, but which can only be explained on the basis of a principle that transcends human nature. These are the "marks" or distinguishing features of the Church. The Church is called one, holy, catholic and apostolic. These characteristics are a sort of sign of the presence of Christ.

To speak of the Church's characteristics in a study of the social nature of man might seem to be off the subject, for we are accustomed to considering them solely from an apologetic point of view. Naturally, the distinguishing features of the Church have their apologetic value also, but their significance, in the first place, is of a metaphysical nature. The true Church is one, holy, catholic and apostolic, not only because in that way it corresponds to the description Jesus gave of it two thousand years ago, but because it has to be like that; this is the natural consequence of the presence of God in a group of associated individuals.

Even those who have only a passing acquaintance with philosophy, will notice at once that such characteristics are in no way arbitrary. God is the One, the True, and the Good; the society which He Himself was to animate could not but be one, true and good.

But although these characteristics are, so to speak, human and visible, they maintain a very close connection with the *invisible* element which animates them. If one looks at the Church under only one of its aspects, either as a merely human society, or as a solely mystical reality, one does violence to the incarnation by separating the human from the divine. The same thing is true when considering the distinguishing marks of the Church.

The Church is *one* (a profound word because the One, in the highest sense, is God). The Church is one in her unity of government which must certainly be understood in a juridical sense. We must not, however, take this to mean a merely bureaucratic subordination of one person to another, for this would destroy the very purpose for which Jesus wished Peter and his successors to have this power of ruling the Church. Jesus sent them out in order that men might learn to know God, to love Him, and to love each other.

The Pope signs himself " the servant of the servants of God, " which is not meant to be a traditional title devoid of any content. It is a title that came spontaneously to the Supreme Pontiffs because their office is to rule in order to give a greater proof of their love. Without the hierarchy, the Church would be a spineless body in which any truly coordinated, organic life would be out of the question. Minus its human aspect, the Church is no longer a body. And without the quickening spirit the body cannot be termed " mystical. "

The Church is also one in the unity of our minds, which have been touched by the hand of God and can therefore henceforward be turned to subjects and themes that are wholly supernatural. This gift, which now lives in us and is perfectly made one with us, with our intellect, is the faith. Oneness in faith is itself also a sign of the presence of Christ among men. Millions of minds cannot think the same way unless one spirit is vivifying and animating them all. Furthermore, unity of faith should not be seen as something that limits our intelligence. The interventions of the hierarchy, of popes and bishops, the " mind of the Church, " are all helpful indications guiding us to the light. To want each person to be free to chose his own private truth is an absurdity on the part of any man, but most of all for the members of the Body of Christ, since Jesus said: " I am the Truth. " [3]

It is also clear that if we are the Body of Christ, there must be the highest, overflowing

---

[3] Jn. 14, 6.

communion between one member and another, between the hierarchy and the faithful, and between diocese and diocese. This, too, is a distinctive mark of the true Church of Christ. It presupposes one hierarchy and one faith. But the unity God produces among the faithful embraces both of these, enveloping all things and all persons. It is charity itself, the bond of all perfection, which flows through the Church of Christ like a river of living water, rendering it a living organism. The mystical Christ is not just an organization, but an organism.

Furthermore, if Christ lives in the Church, if the Holy Spirit is the soul of the Mystical Body, the traces and signs of their presence must be verifiable also in the sanctity of the members' lives. For this reason the Church is *holy*. God, in the infinity of His gifts, distributes graces in souls as He wills, for the good of each and of the whole. Charisms will never be wanting in the Church; they are not a prerogative of the Apostolic first century. Christ has not diminished the divine power which was manifested at His resurrection from the dead. The charisms that are ever present in the Church will continually raise up fresh enterprises, acts of heroism, material deeds of charity, enlightened theologians, new religious orders, lay movements and vocations.

The history of the Church is precisely the history of this presence of Christ, the Sanctifier of men.

Sometimes people are afraid of God's gifts; they fear the deviations and errors which have worked their way into history like the cockle in the good grain. As long as we are on earth, this danger will remain. But to wish to deny the fact of charisms within the Church is to deny implicitly this mysterious presence of Christ, to reduce the Church to a purely human organization, and thus to obstruct the work of the Holy Spirit.

However, if the true Church is the Body of Christ it must be a synthesis of mankind, like Christ Himself. It will have members of all races and nations in its bosom, since it is *universal,* it is *catholic.* United with Christ, all men were present in Him from the first moment of His birth. In the Redemption the complete nature of man offered itself to the Father. This wonderful potentiality, both human and divine, deriving from Christ's individuality and extending itself mystically to the rest of men, must necessarily possess a distinguishing character denoting absolute transcendence over all peoples and nations. The Christian's home country is the Kingdom of Heaven which is open to every man on earth. In the earliest centuries Christians were exceedingly conscious of this. Tertullian, still in the period of persecutions, could say: " We were born yesterday and already we are all over the world. "[4]

But Christ willed also to give each one of us a feeling of direct contact with Him. He willed that there should be someone who could say to us: Christ sent me to you. This would be so through the years and centuries: there would be a mission of Christ containing not only His authority, but also His love. This is the *apostolicity* of the Church which will be transmitted until the last day through the popes and bishops.

Christ thereby rendered Himself so close that one can almost talk with Him. During His life on earth when He sent out His disciples to prepare the kingdom of God, even if they went only a few hours or miles away from the Master, they did not bring the Jewish people as close to Him as do the popes and bishops today. The time separating us from Christ is no longer a few hours, but many centuries; yet the supernatural charism that gets transmitted is animated by realities outside of time and space. Once again in the Church we are face to face with the mysterious presence of Jesus.

---

[4] Tertullian, *Apologeticum,* chap. 37.

For this reason, too, the Church is the true Spouse of the Lamb, completely similar to Him, completely abandoned to, and possessed by Him. She is distinct from her Spouse, but only as Eve was distinct from Adam when in his sleep she was formed by God from his flesh and bone. The Church is flesh of His flesh and bone of His bones.

10 - MANKIND THRIVES IN THE CHURCH

In the past chapters of this brief study we sought to analyze the composition of man. Both experience and philosophy led us to see in man an indivisible unity of soul and body, of spirit and matter. From this is derived his tension toward the all, his innate tendency to go out from his individual self in order to complete himself in union with other men.

We then meditated on the tragic story of man's social nature which, once elevated in Adam, was also wounded in Adam by his disobedience and pride.

Now we would like to examine the extent to which this social tension finds its completion in the Church following the elevation of the whole universe in Christ and the coming into existence of the Mystical Body. We wish to view the Church in its human aspect, that is to say, as a society of human beings. We have already seen that this way of looking at the Church is incomplete, because the Church would not exist were it not sustained by the presence of Christ pervading it. Yet we must also envisage the Church as a society that is humanly complete even at the natural level.

What contribution does the Church make, in this regard, to the life of every man who comes to be a part of it? We know a little of what is received in terms of the life of grace, by means of the sacraments and through the hierarchy, but it is certainly interesting also to analyze this other, human aspect.

At this point, however, we must make a digression to examine the nature of man a little more deeply. We saw that by nature man is social; in other words, he everywhere tends to create a society. The reason for this — as we have seen — is based on those needs which have been implanted in him by the Creator Himself. But of what does this union with other men consist? How do men actually come to form a society?

The image that first comes to mind on hearing the word " society " is that of a plurality of individuals or persons. Even a herd of animals or a flock of sheep is a multitude of individuals; yet they cannot be said to form a society, for this implies intelligent beings who know, and converse with, one another.

Even that is not enough, however, because a group of learned men, all applying their minds to the same work of research, do not constitute a society. Only when they *choose* to arrive at the same goal, at something they have seen or known, and consequently move together in unity of purpose, only then is a society born. The Catholic sociologist Luigi Taparelli sums up his investigations in these words: " society is produced by oneness of end, derived from oneness of knowledge, producing a union of will.... Take away one of these elements and there is no society. " [1]

It is clear that the characteristic features of being — unity, truth, and goodness — are reflected in the constitutive elements of every society: in the end proposed, in knowledge, in the will of its members.

Studying the way in which association between men comes about, we see that it completes individuals precisely through the characteristic elements which are proper to it. The more society is one, the better will it satisfy human needs; the firmer its possession

---

[1] L. Taparelli S. J., *Saggio teoretico di diritto naturale.* Roma, 1949, vol. I, p. 160.

of the truth, the more it will help to strengthen human intelligence; the greater the good it attains, the more perfectly it will satisfy and move the hearts of men. The larger the number of people it succeeds in uniting, the greater fullness of humanity is granted by it to each individual.

At this point we are tempted to apply these standards to the Catholic Church. The Church's unity is perfect, since all its members embrace the same credo under the same Head. The truth illumines " in an equal manner " thousands, millions, and hundreds of millions of people. Faith is a supernatural gift, but it has a human effect as well; it is grafted into the intellect, it thinks with the instruments furnished by man's nature, and even acts as a corrective of our natural intelligence.

When we meet a Japanese Catholic of the new generation, and a Catholic belonging to an ancient French community — two persons, therefore, from highly different cultural experiences, customs and traditions — the unity one senses and breathes is immediate, precisely because the same intellectual realities move their souls and direct even their practical lives. Sharing the same truth makes us one in a way incomparably greater than if we were of the same race or family.

The *good,* too, which is common in the Church to all its members, is a source of the closest union. If we consider it as the end, it is God Himself — God, One and Triune toward whom all of us are tending, both singly and together. In a mysterious and marvelous way this end moves our wills to do what is good. This is the holiness of the Church: holiness of end, of means, and of its members. The experience of doing and willing a good thing together is a very strong tie binding any group of persons to one another.

We see how closely united are those who have striven together for a good and just cause, even on the natural plane; for instance, establishing a scientific discovery or a patent or cure that can benefit humanity. So it is hard to imagine how close a union is effected by the good which Christians together do in the world on the strength of the grace and the sacraments they receive. We are immersed in present-day society, and have no conception of how asocial we would be without the Christian life, the spirit of which invisibly pervades our present society. Only a brusque confrontation with completely a-Christian traditions can reveal to us how much Christianity has contributed by way of justice, equality, abolition of castes, etc., all of which are natural effects of the social development of man brought about by the holiness of the Church.

This becomes all the clearer when we consider that this unity in the *good* and the *true,* which binds Catholics together under one sole hierarchy, reaches out to all the peoples of the earth. This is the catholicity of the Church. When we go to St. Peter's for a solemn public audience, and see the faithful from every part of the globe gathering around the Supreme Pontiff — or when on television we watched the bishops of the entire world assembled in Council — outwardly the joy we feel may seem to be merely fortuitous and superficial, but in fact at that moment our individualism is purged, our provincialism vanishes, our minds open out to vaster problems and our nationalistic sentiments appear as petty as, in effect, they are. In addition to the spiritual graces received we now feel that we are more fully men; we have expanded our souls to the very limits of the earth.

The final characteristic of the Church is apostolicity, which makes us feel that we are members of the Church at a particular historical moment, yet feel spiritually united with all the generations that have preceded us. It carries us back to the moment when Jesus said to the apostles: " As the Father has sent me, I also send you." [2] It grafts me into this visible society, into a whole tradition of which I am an expression: a society which will last till the end of the ages through the mission which, from pope to pope, from bishop to bishop, will go on down the course of history right to the end of time.

In Jesus, moreover, I also feel myself truly linked to the whole of the human race that preceded Him, right back to Adam. The genealogies which the evangelists have transcribed for us place Jesus on a certain point of the line of continuity, but as the fruit of the preceding centuries. If the catholicity of the Church completes me in relation to the men of my own time, the apostolicity of the Church grafts me into the entire course of history.

The coming of Jesus and the founding of the Church also have a natural value, even for all those who will never be members of the Body of Christ, since the effects of this event will spread to all, at least indirectly, and the needs it evokes will be experienced as a boon by all the peoples of the earth. For many it will create a natural predisposition for becoming members of the Body of Christ. In the Mystical Body,

_____

[2] John 20, 21.

through a perfect human society, we are inserted into the divine communion of the Blessed Trinity, a communion that takes us far beyond the actual requirements of our own nature. Our contact with the Trinity is, through Christ and the Church, a reality that is both human and divine.

11 - THE CHRISTIAN AND THE STATE

Christianity presented itself from the start as religious life, as the Church, a human and divine society which has the very lofty end of guiding men to eternal salvation, to the Beatific Vision. The Church was born, however, in the midst of pagan institutions, at a time when the emperor arrogated to himself no less than divine prerogatives. For this reason the words of Paul are all the more astonishing: " Let everyone be subject to the higher authorities, for there exists no authority except from God, and those who exercise it have been appointed by God. "[1] It is thought that these words of the Apostle were written when Nero — the ferocious Nero! — held the imperial scepter in Rome. So they give an indication of the great esteem in which the civil power was held from Apostolic times.

---

[1] Rom., 13, 1.

Perhaps we have formed a false notion of the opposition between the Empire and Christianity, between paganism and martyrdom. The martyrs, the first Christians, were the most faithful subjects of imperial Rome: though they were persecuted, nevertheless they never ceased to recognize and venerate the legitimate power God gave their very persecutors. Tertullian could write in the *Apologeticum:*

> The Christian is the enemy of no one, not even of the emperor whom he knows to have been placed in office by his God, so that he is obliged to love him, to reverence him, to honor him and to desire his safety along with that of the whole Roman Empire. [2]

From that time the doctrine of the two powers, ecclesiastical and civil, was already clear — to be pondered and developed by Catholics throughout the centuries. God in fact, in restoring the human race through Jesus, willed that it should one day return to Him through two authorities, that of the Pope and that of civil rulers, each of which would exercise its powers with a view to its own proper end. The Church's end belongs to the supernatural order, and is based upon a reality, the life of grace, which pervades the souls of men. The civil power, established upon the foundations of the natural

---

[2] *Apologeticum,* 4, 37.

order, has a different goal; it seeks the temporal well-being of its members, human welfare in every sector of social life. The immediate end of civil society is solely temporal, yet this society cannot ignore the fact that man has a destiny superior to nature.

In a well-known document, Pope Gelasius gives us an explanation for this dualism:

> Being aware of human frailty, Christ willed in effect that the authorities to whom power was entrusted for the salvation of the faithful should exist within a wisely ordered society. So He has defined the duties of each power . . . in order that neither might cross the limits of its own sphere, that each might limit itself with modesty to its own role.[3]

Evidently, the Pope cites as the reason for the division of powers the danger ensuing from human frailty, in other words, the fallen nature of man.

To understand still better the difference between the two societies, it is interesting to analyze in what way the authority of each comes from God. In the Pope's case it comes through a direct conferring of powers, of which the proximate efficient cause is Jesus Christ Himself; the cooperation of the Church can enter into the process, in the choice made by the cardinals, but they are only instruments to indicate God's choice. On the other hand, in the natural order,

---

[3] *De anathematis vinculo*, P. L. 59, 108-109.

political power has its justification in God, the author of nature, but its proximate efficient cause is the community of citizens.[4] Consequently, the democratic principle alone does not suffice in the Church, but it is highly to be desired in the civil community.

In the past, even the emperor sometimes called himself the Vicar of Christ, or the Vicar of God, but in an altogether different way from the Roman Pontiff. It is the distinction between the natural sphere and the supernatural that gives us a clear understanding of the difference between the two societies.[5] They constitute, as it were, the soul and body of humanity.

Man's unity is not broken by his being contained in two societies: although he has to participate in the life of the Church and also in that of civil society, he is always, nonetheless, the same individual. Many of man's problems derive from this dual participation because man is one, and yet he feels all the conflicts of the two societies as his own, as things affecting his own person. For this reason it is always desirable to seek harmony, a degree of understanding, a concordat between Church and State, bearing in mind the pre-eminence of the more perfect society,

---

[4] Cf. " Autorità " in the *Enciclopedia Cattolica Italiana,* vol. II, col. 480.

[5] St. Thomas, *De regimine principum,* Bk. I, chap. 14.

the one in which we partake through the gift of grace.

The sense in which the natural society completes each person's individuality follows from these premises. Society is born of nature, as an intrinsic requirement of it; it does not depend on the making of an agreement or contract. It is a requirement of man for his completion in all that concerns the natural life. The life of the family receives support and solace from the civil society; the intelligence and talents of youth are sponsored and helped; economic enterprises, and every other human activity, acquire coordination and stimulation. Not all of this is completely beyond the pale of the Church, for since it is the same individuals that carry on temporal activities while at the same time tending toward their final goal, the Church can and must always express its views, in every field, from a moral and spiritual point of view. But from the technical and political viewpoints, it is up to civil society to set its own norms, autonomously, independent of ecclesiastical authority.

Unfortunately, the history of the relations between the Church and civil society has been one of conflict in the last few centuries. Rationalism attempted to disregard supernatural reality, and hence the Church also. This tends to produce a reaction, in some Christians, of distrust toward the state and its laws [6] — a deleterious tendency because, even if it is understandable psychologically, it has no theological justification. Christians that withdraw from playing their part in civil life and from sincerely observing the laws regulating human relations, renounce the natural development of their humanity, into which grace is engrafted.

A problem much debated today is that of the limits and purposes of state intervention in individual enterprise. The general principle which can guide us, without now going into an inquiry which would lead us away from our main theme, is this: insofar as it is necessary for his completion as an individual, man can and must accept state intervention; but, insofar as such intervention may diminish his personality, he must not tolerate it. Naturally, there can be a variety of applications of this principle and of norms that derive from it. Moreover, communion among men clearly demands authoritative coordination and some degree of intervention which, though it appears restrictive of special interests at times, is nevertheless useful if it tends to the common good.

---

[6] Cf. I. Fuchs S. J. *Auctoritas Dei in auctoritate civili,* in *Periodica de re morali Can. Lit.* T. LII, 1963, P. 15-17.

Particular errors of a doctrinal and moral nature, by now well known, derive for Christians from a false formulation of the problem of the state. Secularism, for instance, presents the reality of life only from a natural point of view, and consequently exalts civil society unduly in people's minds. This error contains its kernel of truth, namely the autonomy of civil society relative to ecclesiastical authority. But, by repudiating the reality of the Church, it ends by actually attributing to the state several prerogatives that really belong to the spiritual order; e. g., the establishing of standards of morality in professional life, or in marriage, education, and so on. It is the modern version of Caesaropapism.

On the other hand, Christians can fail in particular spheres; for example, by adhering to a pseudosupernaturalism, esteeming the theological and supernatural virtues without giving the natural and acquired virtues (like loyalty, justice, and sincerity) proper weight.

The thought turns up in some ancient Christian writers that, unlike the ecclesiastical sphere, civil society on this earth will be divided into states and nations until the end of time. Certainly, up until now even the greatest empires have not withstood time, but have been repeatedly split up and divided. But, on the other hand, man

131

has a natural need for and tendency towards unity, towards the creation of a single society for all men on earth. History presents us with a continual evolution of social forms, starting with the Greek *polis* and arriving at the modern continental and intercontinental federations. Man tries constantly to satisfy his thirst for what is universal even on the natural plane, a thirst which is fully quenched in the Church.

We do not know if this longing will attain its goal, but we hope it shall. It is Christian by nature and casts the light of hope even on all the civil revolutions which a troubled and restless mankind has unleashed in the course of the ages. Let us hope that they are, so to speak, the birth pains — accompanied by God's grace that pervades all things, as the soul fills the body — of a new humanity.

12- THE CHRISTIAN AT WORK
IN THE MYSTICAL BODY

Work first appears in the beginnings of the story of man.[1] It is not, then, an outside addition to man's life. In Genesis it is presented as a necessary part of the corporeal universe. Sacred Scripture says: " There was not yet any field shrub on the earth nor had the plants of the field sprung up, for the Lord God had sent no rain on the earth and there was no man to till the soil . . . ."[2] Labor, along with rain, is here described as a vital factor for the development of the world as such. And then, further on, in another verse it says: " The Lord God took man and placed him in the garden of Eden to till it and to keep it."[3] There was labor, then, even in the earthly paradise.

---

[1] Useful for an understanding of Christian labor is: K. V. Truhlar's *Labor christianus,* Romae, 1961.

[2] Gen. 2, 5.

[3] Gen. 2, 15.

To the contemporary mind, however, working implies painful effort and tedium; it appears as a necessity done more for reasons of survival than for actualizing man's faculties. And freedom from work (relaxation and amusement) is generally thought of in our earthly existence as an oasis of happiness and tranquility. Nevertheless we all know from experience how much boredom can be found in relaxation and amusement. And yet as soon as we return to work, this seems to drop out of mind immediately: toil and effort reappear and we long for the weekend!

Why should labor seem like this if it comes from God and is a natural consequence of human life?

We have already seen how, with original sin, not only the soul of every one of us contracted a stain which can be wiped out only with baptism, but also how the whole universe has been affected by this catastrophe. Man, the prince of creation, rebelled against his God, and all his possessions — the earth and the sea, the animals and the plants — felt the rupture that came about. In their turn they, too, separated themselves from man, though not totally. The plants, animals, and rocks will always, by their very ontological constitution, be at man's service, but they are not as ready to let themselves be manipulated and led as they would have been without the effects of sin. As man has rebelled against God, so, in a certain manner, the universe rebels against man. And the earth, too, has been wounded by sin. Pope Pius XII in one of his allocutions said:

> Before sin, God gave man the earth to cultivate, as the most beautiful and honorable of occupations in the natural order. The actual sins of all men, in addition to the sin of our first parents, have made the curse weigh more heavily on the whole of the earth. The soil, struck by one scourge after another, by floods, earthquakes, plagues and devastating wars, is a sterile, unhealthy desert in some places; and in our days, menaced by terrible weapons of war that lie in wait insidiously for their victims, has refused to bestow its treasures on man spontaneously. The earth is the great casualty, the great victim of all these maladies. [4]

On the other hand, as we have already seen, man must discover his true relationship to nature. He is part of the universe and cannot prescind from the dwelling place that necessarily surrounds him. We have also seen how this determines a sort of intrinsic tension in man by which he longs to make contact with things, to possess, govern and control them.

From this stems the tragedy of labor. We say tragedy, because man's spontaneous inclination

---

[4] Pius XII, Allocution of November 15, 1946, A.A.S. 38 (1946), 434.

is towards looking outside of himself, taking the axe in hand and putting it to the bark. Similarly, material things are, in a sense, naturally inclined to go to man, not guided by intelligence (for they do not possess it) but by their very being. Creation seems to be aware that in man it will find its completion and recapitulation, and that by him it will ultimately be led before God. But this very movement of mutual attraction is hindered by the fact of sin in the world. And so man works, but his experience of work, which all men share, implies pain and travail. Men are the bearers in their lives of an ancient sin, while creation, too, groans in this drama into which it has been unwillingly led to take part. [5]

But into this picture there entered the new element of grace. When God became flesh, He willed to take upon Himself the pains connected with sin, to make them His own in order to do away with them. Jesus is presented in Holy Scripture as a laborer: the son of man and the son of a carpenter. [6] He also willed to experience fatigue. In the course of His apostolic work we find Him, on occasions, tired and in need of rest because, says the Scriptures, He was wearied from the journey.[7] Having taken on man's pains,

---

[5] Cf. Rom. 8, 19-22.
[6] Mt. 13, 55. Cf. also Mk. 6, 3.
[7] Cf. Jn. 4, 6.

He finally experienced death, the culminating act of His work [8] — the work, that is, which the Father had given Him to do.

Jesus had absolute mastery of the universe surrounding Him. This can be seen when He quiets the storm on the lake and when He feeds thousands of persons with a few loaves of bread and a few fish. But ordinarily He did not want to make use of this power during His earthly life. He preferred to appear as one of us. He willed to experience the fatigue that is connected with labor and which has its source in sin. He, who has the unifier *par excellence,* wanted to feel throughout His life, with experimental knowledge, the rupture that had been created between man and material things. In this way He made it His own, thereby making amends for it. In fact, since the time of Jesus, the labor of the Christian is henceforth a sacred act that inserts us in God and leads us on to the Beatific Vision.

The order of grace in which we live has annihilated original sin itself, though not, for the present, its consequences. Henceforth a new life exists within us: unity with the Father has been re-established. A filial relationship brings us back to God. But at the same time we will

---

[8] Cf. Jn. 17, 4.

continue to feel the dividing effects of sin in this world. As it now possesses a remedy, however, this state is no longer cause for endless sorrow, but serves, rather, to feed the flame of charity in our hearts. Thus labor becomes an instrument to help us live in charity. In fact, the subject of this virtue is the will, [9] and, St. Thomas says, " all the habits in our faculties which are moved by a perfect act of the will partake of the form of charity. " [10] Hence also our work, even if not done explicitly as an act of charity, implies an actuation and increase of charity since it is prompted by a Christian will. Naturally this increase of the queen of the virtues will be all the greater the more man directs himself toward God with pure love. And this actualizing of the theological virtue of charity which is implied, cannot come about without the simultaneous actualizing also of the virtues of faith and hope. [11]

Other virtues too, appear in work: in particular, humility. Man feels himself to be before God as a creature before its creator: He experiences his own smallness and the greatness of Him who has so loved him. And he also thereby develops all the virtues that associate

---

[9] Cf. *Summa Theol.* IIa IIae, q. 24, a. 4.
[10] *In III Sent.*, d. 23, q. 3, a. 1.
[11] Cf. Truhlar, *op. cit.*, p. 54.

him with other men. Indeed, work always presupposes the collaboration of others, of those, perhaps, who will later utilize the fruits of our labor. In this way solidarity, patience, altruism, in other words, all the virtues that are the crown and the foundation of fraternal love, come into being and find their proper realization.

This brings the process of the Incarnation into the work of each and every man. By inserting the divine element into what is human, we give even our most insignificant everyday activities a value which will last for all eternity.

All of creation, and not only man, was redeemed at the coming of Jesus. It, too, participates in this intermediate state of preparation for the future kingdom. There is a passage in St. Paul which shows how much the world of irrational beings stands in need of redeemed man:

> The eager longing of creation awaits the revelation of the sons of God. For creation was made subject to vanity — not by its own will but by reason of him who made it subject — in hope, because creation itself also will be delivered from its slavery of corruption into the freedom of the glory of the sons of God. For we know that all creation groans and travails in pain until now.[12]

---

12 Rom. 8, 19-22.

It is in this period that we must prepare the liberation of all creatures through our labor. Creation, too, has been subjected to vanity or, in the words as exegetes interpret it, to sin. Inanimate things are in men's hands, and men can use them either to give glory to God or else to estrange themselves from Him. Nature, moreover, rebels against being used in a way contrary to its purpose, to the end for which it was made. It is now, with the coming of Christianity, that man, making the right use of things and bringing them nearer and nearer to God, is already preparing a new heaven and a new earth.

Henceforth, the highest elevation of inanimate things can be found within the Church itself: the fruits of the soil (bread and grapes) are used to procure the presence of Jesus among men. Water and salt have become means for scattering the blessing of the Most High on the earth and the fields, on factories and schools. Everything re-acquires meaning. Unity has been re-established, though we need to remember that man's absolute dominion over nature has barely begun; it will be complete only at the end of time.

13 – THE NEW HEAVEN AND THE NEW EARTH

It is not easy to speak of the " palingenesis " of the universe: the restoration of the dead and of the material world to new life. It is not easy because the Lord in His infinite wisdom has revealed very little to us about the future life. He knew that we would let ourselves get distracted by useless discussions on the hereafter and might then forget about living a Christian life now in this period of trial. Revelation itself, though diffuse, clear, and precise about everything necessary for living a Christian life, has little information about anything else. It tells us only what is useful here below for living better.

The unconcern, however, of many Christians and in some centuries even of theology itself, with otherworldly problems cannot be justified. Disinterestedness on this subject is not commendable. Even if we are told very little about the hereafter, all the same, the fact that something

145

has been revealed means it must be helpful towards the better understanding of how to prepare ourselves here for our future life. And furthermore, these descriptions show us the importance of our virtues and our intelligence, and the value of external things. If we did not know that our mind and will are destined to possess God with immediate knowledge, neither would we understand the enormous importance of the life of grace which we already have and which is the seed of our future glory.

Until the fourteenth and fifteenth centuries theologians certainly did concern themselves with the future life. From the first Fathers until St. Thomas Aquinas they aways took a loving interest in this problem. But the scientific data they possessed and used at the time (completely inadequate, and to a great extent false) introduced into theological systems many side assertions. With the new scientific discoveries it seemed that even the theological assertions would have to be called into question. In the time of St. Thomas Aquinas, for example, they believed in the Ptolemaic system; they believed in the existence of an empyrean sky; they believed in the existence of bodies that are impure by being composed of heterogeneous elements. From the time that the gratuitousness of these scientific assertions became evident, theologians for centuries no longer dared to deal seriously with the problem of the resurrection of the body and the renewal of the universe.[1]

Only in this century has theology come to realize that this left a serious gap, and that we ought to return to a deeper study of the pertinent parts of revelation, not basing ourselves on systems of physics and chemistry so much as on the principles of philosophy and theology.

The gap which theology had to admit in its system became evident because of the messianic expectations of a renewed earth raised by Marxist-Leninist philosophy. There are people today who talk about an earthly paradise as if it were the logical consequence of the dialectical evolution of society. And even if their assertions can cause many judicious people to smile, in millions of hearts they strike resounding chords, since man (because he is waiting, together with nature, for the renewal of the universe) needs to know something about his future.

That is the reason why it has been necessary to introduce this problem again into the most recent theology,[2] less for scholarly reasons than because we now know that these are among the parts of revelation which are most important for human motivation. They guide men towards their

---

[1] E. Mangenot, *Fin du monde,* D. Th. C., t. X, cols. 25-37.
[2] Cf. H. Verhoeven, *Progrés et redemption cosmique,* P. U. G., Roma, 1959.

end, encouraging them to live a life more consonant with that end, more accurately oriented towards it.

Next to the contemplation of God, in which consists the essential happiness of man, the first truth we find clearly and constantly proclaimed by the Church is the resurrection of the body. It is one of the propositions inserted in the Creed which all Christendom has been repeating for thousands of years and has been singing at Mass on every continent. In his first letter to the Corinthians, St. Paul tells how this resurrection will come about:

> Lo! I tell you a mystery. We shall not all sleep, but we shall all be changed, in a moment, in the twinkling of an eye, at the last trumpet. For the trumpet will sound, and the dead will be raised imperishable, and we shall be changed. For this perishable nature must put on the imperishable, and this mortal nature must put on immortality. [3]

This is an early description of what will happen at the end of the world, when the angels will warn the universe that Jesus is returning. St. Paul feels himself so closely bound to the members of the Body of Christ who will be alive on the last day, that he actually writes, " We

---

[3] 1 Cor. 15, 51-53.

shall not die," though he is not at all sure he will still be alive himself at the time of God's last call. And again in another letter (the first to the Thessalonians) he writes:

> We who live, who survive until the coming of the Lord, shall not precede those who have fallen asleep. For the Lord Himself with cry of command, with voice of archangel, and with trumpet of God will descend from heaven and the dead in Christ will rise first. Then we who live, who survive, shall be caught up together with them in the clouds to meet the Lord in the air, and so we shall ever be with the Lord.[4]

But perhaps the most beautiful description we have of the resurrection of the dead comes from the vision of Ezechiel:

> The hand of the Lord, came upon me, and he led me out in the spirit of the Lord and set me in the center of the plain, which was now filled with bones. He made me walk among them in every direction so that I saw how many they were on the surface of the plain. How dry they were! ... Then he said to me: Prophesy over these bones, and say to them: Dry bones, hear the word of the Lord! Thus says the Lord God to these bones: See! I will bring spirit into you, that you may come to life. I will put sinews upon you, make flesh grow over you, cover you with skin. and put spirit in you so that you may come to life and know that I am the Lord.[5]

---

[4] 1 Thess. 4, 15-17.
[5] Ezek. 37, 1-7.

Also the renewal of the universe is an integral part of our faith. The authority of the Church condemned the theories of a certain Zaninus de Solcia [6] who claimed that

> the world must of its very nature be destroyed and brought to an end, when the humidity of the earth and air is dried up by the heat of the sun, so that the elements will be consumed by fire.

And even earlier, in 553, it was declared in a synod that

> if anyone says the future judgment will be the complete destruction of the physical world, and the end of all will be nature without matter, and in the future there will be nothing material left but only pure spirit, let him be excommunicated.[7]

The same thing had already been said in another way by St. John in the Apocalypse:

> And I saw a new heaven and a new earth. For the first heaven and the first earth passed away, and the sea is no more. [8]

But where the universal catharsis and renewal is revealed more clearly is in the second letter of St. Peter:

> But the heavens that now are and the earth . . . have been stored up, being reserved for fire against the day

---

[6] Denz. 717A.
[7] In: A. Piolanti, *L'al di là,* Torino, 1960, p. 260.
[8] Ap. 21, 1.

of judgment and destruction of ungodly men . . . .
But the day of the Lord will come as a thief; at that
time the heavens will pass away with great violence,
and the elements will be dissolved with heat, and
earth, and the works that are in it, will be burned
up . . . . Await and hasten toward the coming of the
day of God, by which the heavens, being on fire,
will be dissolved and the elements will melt away by
reason of the heat of the fire! But we look for new
heavens and a new earth, according to his promises,
wherein dwells justice. [9]

There is much we can learn from these
statements of St. Peter. First of all, there is
going to be a universal catastrophe, and it will
look as though the planet on which we live and
the stars which surround us are going to disappear
forever. Therefore, there will not be absolute
continuity between matter in this order and
matter in the next. Consequently, the materialistic
progressivism of a terrestrial paradise has nothing
in common with the Christian revelation, as
some had hoped it might; a jump will be made.
But the new state in which the universe will
then exist will be linked to the world which
went before. It has been pointed out that the
word used in the Bible does not mean a newness
of substance, but only a new manner of subsisting
as compared to the way it was. [10]

---

[9] 2 Pet. 3, 7-13.
[10] J. Congar, *Jalons pour une théologie du laïcat*, Paris,
1952, p. 122, note 91.

This elevation of matter will be preceded by a purification which reminds us very much of the Church's authoritative description of purgatory. The epistle of Peter talks of fire which will consume the world and its works, and will enable them to receive divine justice. According to the theological statements of St. Thomas, [11] this purification will remove from the material world the imperfections bequeathed by the sins of men; a great many institutions do in fact bear the traces of the rebellion against God and of sin. From the ruins of the tower of Babel to the latest films from the big movie companies, many human works unfortunately have the stamp of sin upon them. They will all be destroyed.

Furthermore, the whole universe will receive a purification which will be a sort of disposition to receive the glory of God. And this leads at once to another point which seems to be clearly stated in Holy Scripture: paradise will be here on earth; the glorified earth will become the abode of risen humanity. St. John says in the Apocalypse:

> And I saw the holy city, New Jerusalem, coming down out of heaven from God, made ready as a bride adorned for her husband. And I heard a loud voice from the throne saying, " Behold the dwelling of God with men, and he will dwell with them. And they

---

[11] *In IV Sent.* d. 47, q. 11, a. 1, sol. 2.

will be his people, and God himself will be with them as their God . . . ." [12]

Paradise will truly be on earth, or earth in paradise.[13] The opposition between heaven and earth will no longer exist; nor will our vision of God be the least bit disturbed by this transformed existence, since, as St. Thomas says, "He will be everywhere present." [14]

What happened at the Incarnation, the union of the divine with the human, will then be shared by all men and the whole universe. The unity of everything and everyone will find its fullness and its perfection.

---

[12] Ap. 21, 2f.
[13] H. Verhoeven, *op. cit.*
[14] *Suppl.* q. 84, a. 2.

14 - THE LIFE OF MAN IN PARADISE

To try to describe the life of man in paradise is no easy matter. The future life is so different from the present that one runs a great risk of being misunderstood. For example, here on earth we have very clear experience of intellective knowledge. From sensible objects we abstract concepts, we work with them to draw conclusions, make judgments and form connections between them. When we speak of an immediate intuition of something, there has always really been an extremely quick reasoning process underneath it; but it was so imperceptible that we are not even conscious of it ourselves. Accurate analysis, however, will make us realize that an immediate understanding of things outside us is something we do not and cannot have. So, when we describe the heavenly kind of knowledge, the vision of God, we are inclined to project our earthly psychological experience unconsciously into that new mode of existence, into a different kind of life. Now this is justified, up to a point, since it is the same man with the same soul and the same faculties both on earth and in heaven. But none of us has ever had experience of what happens at death: to be totally immersed in God, possessing the *lumen gloriae*. And so the terms we use are the same, since the act of knowledge and the knowing subject both remain the same, but we have to try our hardest to go beyond the experience of our faculties here on earth.

All this is very important, since otherwise there is the opposite danger of being completely negative, or, in other words, of considering life in the hereafter so totally different from life on earth that there would be nothing at all in common between them.

We will undergo a transformation, but not such, as we shall see later, as to annihilate the essential acts of human life. But these will be performed in a way too different for us even to be able to imagine it now.

What has been defined and is therefore sure Catholic doctrine is the vision of God, which gives an immediate and direct[1] perception of

---

[1] A. Piolanti, *L'al di là,* Torino, 1960, p. 217: " Not only is God completely immaterial: God has no potentiality, He

the divine essence, granting our souls eternal beatitude and rest. It is our spiritual faculties, intelligence and will, that will be activated. There will still be love in paradise, though it will no longer be meritorious; the knowledge peculiar to the *lumen gloriae* is outside all our present experience, but theologians say [2] that the cognitive acts to which we were accustomed on earth will not be destroyed. We will not only be endowed with infused knowledge, which the saints in their earthly existence could have already experienced, [3] but even our acquired knowledge will not be lost, nor cease developing, " so the soul can always progress... by means of reasoning, elaborating the perceptions of this and of the future life. " [4]

As for sense knowledge, that too will continue after the resurrection of the body. [5] It will not attain God who is pure spirit, of course, but it can reach the physical realities in

---

is pure act, He is Being by His essence. His intelligibility is the same as His being; and so the being and intelligibility of God are convertible. He is Being, but because He is the pure act of being, He is thought. Aristotle said *nòesis noèseos,* or the thought of thought. The divine essence, therefore, being thought as much as being, can unite itself directly to the intellect elevated by the *lumen gloriae* and actuate it conceptually, or in other words make it know."

[2] *Summa Theol.* I, q. 89, a. 6.
[3] D. Bertetto, *Gesú Redentore,* Florence, 1958, pp. 295-296.
[4] D. Bertetto, *op. cit.,* p. 296.
[5] *Suppl.* q. 92, a. 2.

paradise, like, for example, the glorified bodies of
Jesus, of Mary, and of the other saints. Therefore,
we will continue to use the senses like sight,
hearing, smell, taste, and touch. [6] They will also
provide us with a way of perceiving God's
presence in all things. As on earth we can tell
through our senses that something is alive, so we
shall in paradise be able to enjoy the presence of
God in material things even through our senses
(being aware of His presence also independently
of them). Thomas Aquinas, whose doctrine is
a summary of medieval theology on this subject,
rules out all forms of material food, although
he admits the sense of taste. He says that
food is connected with the imperfection of man
and not with his essential qualities: food is
needed only on earth, to keep man alive, but
where life is eternal there is no need of food. [7]
In paradise, for the same reason, bodies
" neque nubent neque nubentur " [8]; generative
life is also bound up with a human imperfection,
the need to complete the individual in the
species. This need will not exist in heaven,
having been fulfilled through the perfection of
humanity and the enrichment which that perfection will confer on each individual.[9]

---

[6] *Suppl.* q. 82, a. 4.
[7] *Loc. cit.*
[8] Mt. 22, 30.
[9] *Suppl.* q. 81, a. 4.

All this is more the teaching of theologians than dogma. The Church has not defined anything on the subject. But it has stated clearly that the virtues will continue to exist in the soul, although they will acquire no additional merit. We know that faith and hope will cease in paradise. They are too bound up with this world's mode of existence; God's presence will do away with all need of them. But charity will continue. There is also a decree of the Church on the existence of the moral virtues in heaven. The Council of Siena condemned Abelard for excluding " chaste fear " from the future world. [10] St. Thomas says, too, that all the cardinal virtues will continue in the heavenly country, [11] but so penetrated by the divine that they will be indistinguishable from the gifts of the Holy Spirit, which will not be lost. [12] Since there are physical bodies, there will still be space, motion, and time. [13] This will all coexist with divine eternity which will penetrate everything.

After making these clarifications we can deal with the two problems which particularly interest us. First of all, will there still be labor in the kingdom of heaven? To begin, we must explain what we mean by labor. If we associate with the

[10] Denz. 382.
[11] *Summa Theol.* IIa IIIae, q. 52, a. 3 ad 2.
[12] *Suppl.* q. 16, a. 2.
[13] *Suppl.* q. 84, a. 3.

concept of labor that of material fatigue, toil, and pain, it must obviously be excluded from the place of delight where all is joy. But in the analysis made in the foregoing chapters, we have seen that work does not necessarily mean pain: pain is a result of original sin. Of its nature, work is the relationship of men with external things; it is the act of the rational creature's mediation for the elevation of the world of the irrational to give glory to God. Taken in its essential elements, it seems to us that such a relationship between man and created things will continue even after the end of the world. To be immersed in nature is part of the physical makeup of man. It is part of the metaphysical constitution of material things that they tend toward man in order to give formal glory to God, a true and full glory. And so it is not surprising if we find affirmations of this sort in contemporary theology.[14] De Guibert, the great writer of mystical theology, says:

> Perhaps, during our earthly pilgrimage, we will have to sacrifice some considerable artistic or scientific abilities, and to mortify some attitudes which could not but have enriched and elevated our life . . .; but this will not have been definitive, and in our risen bodies

---

[14] Truhlar, *Labor christianus,* Roma, 1961, p. 121 ff; Thils, *Théologie des réalités terrestres,* Bruges, 1946, pp. 168-169; G. De Guibert, *Leçons de Théologie spirituelle,* I, pp. 205-206.

and the society of our brethren who have risen with us, those same abilities (intensified and elevated) will be fully and completely fulfilled. We know nothing at all about what music and literature there will be in heaven: what is certain is that this feeling for beauty, even for the sensible beauty to which those activities are directed, far from disappearing will be developed there as it finds worthy objects that give it complete satisfaction.[15]

The other problem is that of our sociality. We have seen that this human need is taken care of here on earth through two societies, the Church and the State. But it is easy to understand that, as they appear to us now, these things are bound up profoundly with our temporary and sinful existence.

Civil society is going to disappear;[16] it is only useful for this life. Perhaps the social virtues will remain: like civic love, for instance, which might make people feel united to one another even in heaven, though without its present limitations and insularity. And yet, even if there will be something left which will remind us of civil life, it will then be joined and unified in Jesus. Christ will be in the fullness of His splendor as Head, as Priest, and as King. He is the center of heaven.

15 De Guibert, *op. cit.,* pp. 205-206.
16 *Suppl.* q. 98, a. 1 ad 3.

Nor can the Church continue as it is organized here below. What purpose would the hierarchy and the sacraments serve in heaven, where Christ the Head is visible and God is present in everything and everyone? The reality of the mystical Christ, however, which makes the Church what it is and gives it its earthly characteristics of being one, holy, catholic, and apostolic, is certainly going to last. In heaven only Christ and His Mystical Body will live, in a way that will be simultaneously divine and human, with the Trinitarian sociality finding its outward expression in glorified humanity. This is the Church triumphant.

To try to give a more detailed description of the beatitude which will come to us from our incorporation into Christ would be to attempt the impossible. St. Paul was transported by God to its contemplation, but could not describe it when he came back as a mortal among mortals; it is too far above our meager words and feeble intelligence.

15 - MARY, THE "TYPE" OF SOCIETY

It is truly surprising how the Church's mysterious instinct uses texts of Holy Scripture for the liturgy of the Blessed Virgin which a layman could think unsuitable for singing the greatness of an individual person, even one as exalted as the Blessed Virgin Mary. For instance, for the Epistle on the 8th of December, a passage from the Book of Proverbs is read which runs:

> The Lord begot me, the first-born of his ways, the forerunner of his prodigies of long ago; from of old I was poured forth, at the first, before the earth. When there were no depths I was brought forth, when there were no fountains or spring of water; before the mountains were settled into place, before the hills, I was brought forth.[1]

And the Introit for the Mass of the Assumption quotes the twelfth chapter of the Apocalypse:

---

[1] Proverbs 8, 22-25.

A great sign appeared in heaven: a woman clothed with the sun, and the moon was under her feet, and upon her head a crown of twelve stars.

Do not these phrases seem to fit the Mystical Body, the Church, better than Mary? How have they stayed in use for centuries? Why have the Christian people not only felt no uneasiness with these texts but even fed upon them? How did they find perfect harmony between these texts and that mysterious reality which is Our Lady? This leads to the question of the relationship between Mary and the Church.

Only in the last century has theology begun to cast some light on this relationship, especially in the last few years since the doctrine of the one Body of Christ has again become of current interest. But theologians have not yet succeeded in producing anything profound or definitive. Towards understanding Mary's greatness under a new light, no more has been made than a loving approach.

Some theologians think that Catholic Mariology, compared with other treatises, lacks depth in positive theology; they think that affection rather than speculation has guided our attitude towards the Blessed Virgin. Let us see whether reason and positive sources agree with what liturgy and piety say about Mary.

Among the Fathers speculating on the relationship between Mary and the Church, St. Ambrose makes the first clear affirmation asserting that " Mary is the type of the Church. " [2] He makes a comparison between the virginity of Mary and that of the Church, and between Mary's motherhood and the Church's.[3] The same concepts are found in St. Augustine.

The expression, "Mary, type of the Church," later enjoyed an unforeseen popularity. In the Middle Ages theologians great and small develop the concept, beginning with St. Peter Damian, who asserts, " The entire universal Church is modeled after her who is the Mother of the Christ," [4] down to Herveus Natalis Brito who declares, " The Church is formed in imitation of the Mother of its Lord," [5] and on to Honorius of Autun who repeats that " The glorious Virgin Mary was a type of the Church. " [6]

Nevertheless, in presenting Mary as an image

---

[2] " Bene desponsata, sed virgo, quia est Ecclesiae typus, quia est immaculata sed nupta. Concepit nos virgo de Spiritu, parit nos virgo sine gemitu. Et ideo fortasse sancta Maria alii nupta, ab alio repleta, quia et singulae Ecclesiae Spiritu quidem replentur et gratia, iunguntur tamen ad temporis speciem sacerdoti " (St. Ambrose, *In Lucam* II, 7 CSEL, 32-4, 45).

[3] Cf. Vatican II, *Dogmatic Constitution of the Church,* No. 63f.

[4] *De horis canonicis,* cap. IV, P. L. 145, 226.

[5] *In Ep. II ad Cor.,* P. L. 181, 1097.

[6] *Sigillum Mariae,* P. L. 172, 499.

of the Church the medieval writers limit themselves to acknowledging certain similarities and points of contact, rather than thoroughly investigating what lies behind the similarity. Theirs is theology touching on great truths, but sensing more than demonstrating them. Just the image alone, however, already says something.

The word " type " does not just mean an outline or model. It is a word used by St. Paul to refer to figures of the Old Testament which would find their reality in the New. The medieval theologians certainly used the word in this sense, too; but they added something. To them Mary was not just a symbol, she was a complete exemplar to which the Church itself must look.[7] Mary as " type " of the Church was the perfect ideal, which would ever remain unattainable but which the Church could always approach.[8] For them the loftier of the two terms of comparison was Mary, not the Church; this was not true of the " types " of the Old Testament. The medieval theologians saw a relationship, above all, under the aspects of Mary's motherhood, virginity, sanctity, and faith. From Mary's motherhood, in fact, a very special relationship to human society can be inferred:

---

[7] Cf. Vatican II, *Dogmatic Constitution of the Church*, No. 64.

[8] *Ibid.,* 65.

170

like the Church, she, too, is the spiritual mother of all men. [9]

Her human fullness must therefore have been perfect if it is true that man finds his full human development through his union with others. Because Mary is very closely related to every one of us, she must have possessed such a social sense as can never again be equaled.

Mary is further presented as the miniature of the whole Church. She possesses as much as, indeed more than, the total supernatural life of all its members taken singly or collectively. Pope Pius XII says, in his encyclical *Mystici Corporis*: " May the Virgin Mother of God obtain for all of us a genuine love for the Church, she whose most holy soul was filled with the divine spirit of Jesus Christ more than are all other souls put together. "

Until now, the study of the relationship between Mary and the Church has presented to our thoughts Mary, a person — whereas the Church is a collectivity. But is there more to say? Can it be held that Mary is the summing up and the personification of the Church itself?

---

[9] *Ibid.*, 53f.

Do the statements which have been made by contemporary writers: " Mary and the Church ... are, in a way, the same mystery viewed under two different aspects " [10] and " All of the Church is in Mary, " [11] correspond to a reality in the soul of Mary ?

We can certainly answer that they do. First of all because, during the months when the Saviour was carried in the Blessed Virgin's womb as in a tabernacle, the statement, " All of the Church is in Mary, " had its greatest reality and most sublime actuation. Together with Jesus we were all present there, united mystically in His body. [12]

But it is not for this reason alone. God willed by a mysterious decree that the Virgin's *fiat* to the angel should be the reply of human nature to its Creator: Mary included in that " yes " the " yes " that all of us would repeat after her. St. Thomas understood this clearly when he said that she spoke " to show the spiritual marriage between the Son of God and the human creature: and therefore at the Annunciation the consent of the Virgin was sought *loco totius humanae natu-*

[10] Cf. Card. Suenens, *Teologia dell'apostolato,* Roma, 1953, p. 226.

[11] Dillenschneider, *Marie et l'Eglise,* Paris, 1953, III, 128.

[12] Cf. St. Pius X, *Ad diem laetissimum,* A.A.S. 30, pp. 452-453.

rae, " [13] which means as a representative of all human nature. This statement of St. Thomas has been repeated by many Popes, among them Pius XII in the encyclical *Mystici Corporis,* giving it the added weight of papal authority. [14]

This same mysterious reality is true also at the foot of the cross: there, too, we were spiritually present in Mary. Theology will clarify this in time, as the Blessed Virgin is considered not only as mother but as spouse: as such, she is the personification of the Church.

In the sixteenth century, we find Salmeron summing up previous writers' interpretations of Jesus' words, " Woman, behold thy son, " and saying that Jesus on the cross " calls her woman, because in the mysteries she was not considered as mother but as the second spouse, in contrast to the first spouse, Eve. " [15] The same line of thought was followed by others, among them Scheeben and Olier. By now it is widely taught that " the *fiat* of the sorrowful heart of Mary on Calvary was obviously also a *fiat* uttered in the name of all humanity to be saved, a *fiat* of universal, representative validity. " [16]

---

[13] *Summa Theol.* III, q. 30, a. 1.
[14] Leo XIII declares this expression " most true " in the encyclical *Octobri mense.*
[15] *Comm. in Ev. Hist.,* vol. VI, p. 39, Cologne, 1602.
[16] Dillenschneider, *op. cit.,* p. 124.

Mary appears as the personification of the whole Church even more at the Assumption. As we know, the resurrection of the body follows an inverse movement to that of original sin: while the latter " goes from human nature to individuals, regeneration in Christ goes from individual persons to the nature, so that when all individuals have been saved, human nature itself will be capable of salvation and resurrection." [17] For this reason the whole Church will rise at the end of time in collective fullness. But the final resurrection of the Christian collectivity is already personified in Mary, assumed in glory into heaven. [18]

She is already the " pleroma " of Christ.

The dialectic which Adam and Eve had started in the world (individual society), finds in Mary its definitive synthesis: a synthesis of the earth joined with heaven, a complement and reflexion of the synthesis of heaven and earth in Christ.

---

[17] Ch. Journet, *Marie est au coeur de l'Eglise,* in *Nova et Vetera,* 1950, pp. 110-111.

[18] Dillenschneider, *op. cit.,* p. 127.

16 - THEOLOGY AND LIFE

We have now finished our rapid survey of theology looking at the two aspects of human reality which are receiving greater attention and study today: sociality and labor. We have seen how they derive from man himself as created by God: man who has been put into the universe and made part of it, in touch with material things; man who has a physical need to seek self-fulfillment in a woman and in other men. He has relations with others which are not superficial, even though his spiritual soul makes him independent and superior to all since it joins him directly with God. Man has bonds with the world around him and with the society which receives him.

As we have seen, his dynamic tensions are three: towards heaven, towards mankind, and towards material things; these, however, join each other, interlace, and form into the one movement of the universe and of mankind towards God.

Therefore, there would have been a marvelous harmony in creation, even without grace. The love of God and the contemplation of the universe would have filled men with a natural happiness. But the Blessed Trinity willed more: it willed to elevate all this; it willed to share the divine nature with man. The river which flowed into humanity from the heart of God raised the cosmos precisely because man was related to the whole. This was the earthly paradise, a sublime reflection of God's love.

With his sin, man broke the harmony, took away the supernatural reality from the world, and marred the very nature of things; he began suffering and dying. But heaven permitted this in order that God's infinite love might be made even more manifest. The second Person of the Trinity, the Word, willed to unite Himself to human nature. A wonderful mystery, because, by becoming related to us, He took pain, the consequence of sin, upon Himself. For this reason He experienced suffering and death; He experienced the break that had come about in nature also. But the hypostatic union between Creator and creature brought back the human and corporeal universe onto a divine plane.

Everything becomes a continuation of Christ — men form His Mystical Body, even material things have meaning only in Jesus, and all becomes deified. Since Christ is risen, men will rise; since Christ is risen, even earthly reality, being transformed, will remain at the end of time. Consequently Christ is the alpha and omega; Christ is the efficient cause which gives us life and the final cause to which we all tend. And Christ will be the profound reality pervading us even before the last day. Because of our small mentality we have had to give images and names, which logically are human, to supernatural society into which we are received here on earth. We talk about law, and forms, etc., but they are only the external signs of Christ's presence pervading the Church. The Church is the sacrament of Christ; it cannot exist apart from Him. Losing ourselves in it, we find ourselves again in Jesus, we rediscover ourselves in the Blessed Trinity.

The marvelous experiences of Catherine of Siena, Teresa of Avila, John of the Cross, and Francis of Assisi are the typical experiences of the Church. They immersed themselves fully in an earthly society containing bishops and popes who were mediocre or sinful, and into forms of ecclesiastical life tied to those of the world and the times in which they lived, which would be repugnant to us now; however, while accepting all that, they had direct contact with Christ who lives in the Church beyond its forms and appearances, and beyond men's sins. Some found themselves in direct conversation with the Trinity, others experienced a special love for each of the Three Divine Persons, and still others received a marriage ring or the stigmata directly from Jesus.

Christ dominates history. That history which seems to us to pass so slowly, made up of so many small things, is, in reality, the history of the life of Jesus in men. It is the irresistible progress of mankind towards becoming Him. The revolutions which occasionally trouble the surface of this progress, the so-called great revolutions of mankind which terrify or attract men's minds for several decades and seem to leave a deep impression on human history, are only marginal episodes in the progress of man towards Christ. Men may seek to get in its way, and try to stop the river; but after a few years we find that the dams themselves, even the strongest of them, have become part of the river, enlarging it and increasing its power; combining with the rest, they too plunge on towards the divine sea.

After all, even evil is permitted by God; in fact, He actually makes use of it.

History now has meaning; it makes constant progress, no longer in cycles as in the pagan idea of an everlasting, endless repetition. We know who is the end of history, and history's Lord.

This vision which reaches from creation to the last day must not make us forget the present — the little day-by-day present which seems to sadden and shrink us, the little present time made of physical and family sufferings, the little present made of economic worries and work. The two realities, the universal and the particular, are not separate at all. It is possible for us to live the greatest truths of the Church in the midst of ordinary everyday worries. This is the marvel of Christianity.

Sometimes people have wanted to idealize the saints, removing them from our banal world into an eternal world of all-perfect ideas, all changeless, all far from the petty surroundings which disturb us and would have withered even the greatest men. This is wrong. Those saints, the great personalities of Christian history, grew up in the midst of precisely those small, thorny things of every day, those thorny things which touched them, and pricked them, and sometimes drew their blood. They found themselves in the mainstream of the history of Christ in the world just because they did not abandon their environment and their time. They were immersed in it. Whoever has wished to depict them as far-removed from reality, whoever has tried to idealize them by detaching them from what is contingent, has mutilated their Christianity. They have drawn beautiful pictures but not Christian saints. One of the propositions of the Creed is just this: " Jesus was born of the Virgin Mary and suffered under Pontius Pilate. " The Trinity chose to meet men in a particular moment of history, at a particular point on the earth.

And so, the realities of human life, social life and labor, are not obstacles to a Christian, but are his normal habitat where he carries on the Incarnation.

Many are tempted to look for sanctity " somewhere else, " attempting to evade the very difficulties which could make us Christians and make us saints. There are times when one must flee from difficulties, but they are very few. The general rule of accepting our day-to-day toil is valid for all.

It is then that the Incarnation is repeated spiritually, and the Word is made flesh mystically, perhaps in some work, or in a gesture, or maybe in a smile. The gesture, work, or smile is deified by Christ and made eternal.

But there is one particular action which more than any other opens our soul to infinity, and more than any other sums up for us all Christian history, and all natural history, the creation of the world and of man, the death and sufferings of Jesus, and the recapitulation of the universe. It is an action which makes Jesus Himself present to us. This is the actualization of His words: "I have a new commandment to give you, that you are to love one another; that your love for one another is to be like the love I have borne you." [1]

This reciprocal action of man is all-inclusive; and so it is *His* commandment. The human universe, which develops through mutual charity and sublimates social tension, is embraced by it. The corporeal universe is embraced by it since things find their true meaning by being used in active charity; the cup of water given to the thirsty (which I will get back in paradise) besides sanctifying me, also ennobles matter, restoring it to man, who in turn brings it to God. In mutual charity everything acquires a Christian flavor. The word "charity" has been lived so badly, and been so abused, that now the masses no longer recognize it. They associate it with the conceited attitude of one who does not care about others enough to see them as himself, but contents himself with giving them a crumb or two. But true Christian charity, on the other hand, wants all men equal to oneself, in hopes of establishing with them a society, the focusing in time and space of the greatest human and divine society, the Church.

---

[1] Jn. 13, 34.

To live mutual charity is "to be the Church," at work, in the family, or in school. It is the church-community that one is setting out to live. The Christianity for which we are criticized today is certainly Christianity made up of divine realities — sacraments and sermons — but not of divine *life*.

And the Life, that life which is Jesus, is present in the mutual exchange of love between men. He, in fact, has promised to be present in a special way to whomever lives like this: " Where two or three are gathered together in my name, I am there in the midst of them. " [2] It is also the will of Jesus, who is eternally present in the life of the Church, to be present whenever two or three Christians decide to " be the Church," wherever they are, be it in a prison or a factory, at school or in the marketplace.

It is the wish of Him who created the universe to pervade our short lives, our days of misery, and our hard work.

He who is the Recapitulator of the universe, and the hidden Reality within history, is present when two children, at play in a nursery school, decide to love one another as Jesus loves them.

---

[2] Mt. 18, 20.

WORKS CONSULTED

ST. AMBROSE, *In Lucam*, P.L. 15.

ST. AUGUSTINE, *Ep.* 185, P.L. 33.

ST. AUGUSTINE, *Enarr. in Psalmos*, 31, P.L. 36.

ST. AUGUSTINE, *Enarr. in Psalmos*, 70, P.L. 36.

ST. CYRIL OF ALEXANDRIA, *In Johannem*, P.G. 74.

GELASIUS, *De anathematis vinculo*, P.L. 59, cols. 108-109.

HERVEUS NATALIS BRITO, *In Ep. II ad Cor.*, P.L. 181.

ST. HILARY, *Tractatus in Psalmos*, 125, P.L. 9.

HONORIUS OF AUTUN, *Sigillum Mariae*, P.L. 172.

ST. JOHN DAMASCENE, *De fide orth.*, Bk. III, P.G. 94.

ST. JOHN DAMASCENE, *Hom. de Transfig. Dom.*, P.G. 96, cols. 791-804.

ST. JOHN OF THE CROSS, *Salita al monte Carmelo*, Bk. II, Roma, 1940 (E. tr. *Ascent of Mount Carmel*, London, 1934).

ST. PETER DAMIAN, *De horis canonicis*, P.L. 145.

TERTULLIAN, *Apologeticum*, P.L. 1.

ST. THOMAS AQUINAS, *Scriptum super sententias*, Paris, 1956.

ST. THOMAS AQUINAS, *Compendium theologiae*, in *Opuscola theologica*, vol. I, Torino, 1954.

ST. THOMAS AQUINAS, *De regimine principum*, Torino, 1948.

ST. THOMAS AQUINAS, *Expositio in Psalmos*, 21, Romae, 1570.

ST. THOMAS AQUINAS, *Summa Theologica*, III and Supplementum, Torino, 1948.

ANGER, J., *La doctrine du Corps mystique de Jésus-Christ d'après les principes de la théologie de S. Thomas*, Paris, 1952.

BANDAS, R., *La Redenzione*, Roma, 1961.

BENOIT, P., O.P., *Corps, Tête et plérôme dans les épîtres de la Captivité*, in *Exégèse et théologie*, vol. II, Paris, 1961.

BERTETTO, DOMENICO, *Gesú Redentore*, Firenze, 1958.

CERFAUX, *La théologie de l'Eglise suivant Saint Paul,* Paris, 1948 (E. tr. *The Church in the Theology of St. Paul,* St. Louis and London, 1959).

CHARDON, LOUIS, *La Croix de Jésus,* Paris, 1937.

CHENU, M.D., O.P., *Pour une théologie du travail,* Paris, 1955.

CONGAR, YVES, O.P., *Jalons pour une théologie du laïcat,* Paris, 1952 (E. tr. *Lay People in the Church,* Westminster, Md., 1957).

CONGAR, YVES, O.P., *Le Christ, Marie et l'Eglise,* Paris, 1955 (E. tr. *Christ, Our Lady, and the Church,* Westminster, Md., 1957).

CONGAR, YVES, O.P., *Le mystère du Temple,* Paris, 1958 (E. tr. *The Mystery of the Temple,* Westminster, Md., 1962).

DE GUIBERT, J., S.J., *Leçons de théologie spirituelle,* vol. I, Toulouse, 1955.

DE LAGARDE, G., *La naissance de l'esprit laïque,* vol. I-II, Louvain, 1956.

DE LUBAC, HENRY, S.J., *Catholicisme,* Paris, 1952 (E. tr. *Catholicism,* New York, 1950).

DILLENSCHNEIDER, *Toute l'Eglise en Marie,* in *Marie et l'Eglise,* 1953.

DURWELL, F.X., *La résurrection de Jésus, Mystère de salut,* Paris, 1961 (E. tr. *The Resurrection,* New York, 1960).

FLICK, S.J. - ALSZEGHY, S.J., *Il Creatore,* Firenze, 1961.

FORESI, PASQUALE, *La Passion de Jésus, mystère d'amour* in *Assemblées du Seigneur,* Bruges, 1963.

FUCHS, J., S.J., *Le droit naturel,* Paris, 1960.

GALTIER, P., S.J., *De incarnatione ac redemptione,* Paris, 1947.

GALTIER, P., S.J., *Les deux Adam,* Paris, 1947.

GARRIGOU-LAGRANGE, R., O.P., *L'altra vita e la profondità dell'anima,* Brescia, 1947.

GARRIGOU-LAGRANGE, R., O.P., *De Christo Salvatore,* Torino, 1949.

GILLEMANN, G., *Il primato della carità in teologia morale,* Brescia, 1959.

GOFFI, TULLO, *Laicità politica e Chiesa,* Roma, 1960.

GUERRY, E., *Dans le Christ ttotale,* Bruges, 1952.

GUTZWILLER, R., *Herr der Herrscher,* Einsiedeln, 1951.

HERIS, C.V., O.P., *Il Mistero di Cristo,* Brescia, 1945.

JOURNET, CHARLES, *Marie est au coeur de l'Eglise,* in *Nova et Vetera,* 1950.

JOURNET, CHARLES, *L'Eglise du Verbe incarné,* 2 vols., Paris, 1951.

KASEL, ODO, *Mysterium der Ekklesia,* Mainz, 1961.

LABOURDETTE, M.M., O.P., *Le péché originel et les origines de l'homme*, Paris, 1953.

LEO XIII, Encyclical letter *Octobri mense*, A.S.S., 1891.

MANGENOT, E., *La fin du monde*, in D.Th.C., vol. X, cols. 25-37.

MARITAIN, J., *Umanesimo integrale*, Roma, 1946 (E. tr. *True Humanism*, New York, 1938).

MARITAIN, J., *L'homme et l'Etat*, Paris, 1953 (E. tr. *Man and the State*, Chicago, 1951).

MERSCH, EMILE, S.J., *Le Corps mystique du Christ*, 2 vols., Paris, 1951.

MERSCH, EMILE, S.J., *La théologie du Corps mystique*, 2 vols., Paris, 1954 (E. tr. *The Theology of the Mystical Body*, St. Louis, 1951).

MERSCH, EMILE, S.J., *Morale et Corps mystique*, Paris, 1955 (E. tr. *Morality and the Mystical Body*, New York, 1939).

MERSCH, EMILE, S.J., *Le Christ, l'homme et l'univers*, Paris, 1962.

PARENTE, PIETRO, *Teologia viva*, vol. I: *Il mistero di Cristo*, Roma, 1954.

PARENTE, PIETRO, *L'io di Cristo*, Brescia, 1955.

PARENTE, PIETRO, *De Verbo Incarnato*, Romae, 1956.

PIOLANTI, ANTONIO, *Corpo mistico e Sacramenti*, Roma, 1955.

PIOLANTI, ANTONIO, *Maria e il Corpo mistico*, Roma, 1957.

PIOLANTI, ANTONIO, *Il mistero della Comunione dei Santi*, Roma, 1957.

PIOLANTI, ANTONIO (edited by), *L'Al di là*, Torino, 1960.

PIUS X, Encyclical letter *Ad diem illum laetissimum*, A.S.S., 1904.

PIUS XI, Encyclical letter *Lux veritatis*, A.A.S., 1931.

PIUS XII, Encyclical letter *Humani generis*, A.A.S., 1950.

PRAT, I., S.J., *La teologia di S. Paolo*, 2 vols., Torino, 1943 (E. tr. *The Theology of St. Paul*, 2 vols, London, 1926, 1927).

RAHNER, K., S.J., *Ecrits théologiques*, 2 vols, Bruges, 1959.

RAHNER, K., S.J., *Marie, Mère du Seigneur*, Paris, 1960.

ROSCHINI, GABRIELE, *La Mariologia di S. Tommaso*, Roma, 1950.

SALMERON, *Comm. in Ev. Hist.*, vol. IV, Colonia, 1602.

SCHEEBEN, M.J., *I Misteri del Cristianesimo*, Brescia, 1960 (E. tr. *The Mysteries of Christianity*, St. Louis and London, 1946).

SCHEEBEN, M.J., *La Mère virginale du Seigneur*, Paris, 1953.

SUENENS, CARD. LÉON-JOSEPH, *Teologia dell'apostolato*, Roma, 1953.

TAPARELLI, LUIGI, *Saggio teoretico di Diritto naturale*, 2 vols., Roma, 1949.

THILS, GUSTAVE, *Théologie des réalités terrestres*, 2 vols, Paris, 1946.

THILS, GUSTAVE, *Théologie et réalité sociale*, Paris, 1952.

Tromp, Sebastiano, S.J., *Corpus Christi quod est Ecclesia*, 3 vols., Romae, 1946-1960.

Truhlar, Carolus, S.J., *Labor christianus*, Romae, 1961.

Verhoeven, Enrico, *Progrés et redemption cosmique*, P.U.G., Roma, 1959.

Welty, *Gemeinschaft und Einzelmensch*, Salzburg, 1935.

Zapelena, T., S.J., *De Ecclesia Christi*, 2 vols., Roma, 1954.

Katholischer Katechismus, 1960.

Various Authors, *Eglise et apostolat*, Tournai, 1957.

Various Authors, *Maria et Ecclesia*, vol. III: *De parallelismo Mariam inter et Ecclesiam*, Roma, 1959.

Vatican II, *Pastoral Constitution on the Church in the Modern World*.
Dogmatic Constitution on the Church.
Decree on Ecumenism.
Decree on Eastern Catholic Churches.